NICK DRAKE

T0269874

The Reverb series looks at the connections between music, artists and performers, musical cultures and places. It explores how our cultural and historical understanding of times and places may help us to appreciate a wide variety of music, and vice versa.

reverb-series.co.uk
Series editor: John Scanlan

Already published

The Beatles in Hamburg
Ian Inglis

Van Halen: Exuberant California, Zen Rock'n'roll
John Scanlan

Brazilian Jive: From Samba to Bossa and Rap
David Treece

Tango: Sex and Rhythm of the City
Mike Gonzales and Marianella Yanes

Nick Drake: Dreaming England
Nathan Wiseman-Trowse

Remixology: Tracing the Dub Diaspora
Paul Sullivan

NICK DRAKE

DREAMING ENGLAND

NATHAN WISEMAN-TROWSE

REAKTION BOOKS

For Kelly and Harry

Published by Reaktion Books Ltd
33 Great Sutton Street
London ECIV ODX, UK
www.reaktionbooks.co.uk

First published 2013

Printed and bound in Great Britain by Bell & Bain, Glasgow

A catalogue record for this book is available from the British Library

ISBN 978 1 78023 176 1

CONTENTS

Nick by Keith Morris, London, August 1970.

INTRODUCTION

On the edge of a field of corn, in the shade of an oak tree, two young men, one reclining against the trunk, the other lying at the foot of the tree, smoke cigarettes and gaze up at the summer morning sky. Dappled sunlight filters through the leaves above their heads. The blond youth gazing up at the sky is Sebastian Flyte, the dissolute progeny of the aristocratic Marchmain family. His companion, who seems somewhat less impressed by the bucolic scene than by his charismatic companion, at whom he gazes wistfully, is Charles Ryder.

> We ate strawberries and drank the wine. As Sebastian promised, they were delicious together. The fumes of the sweet, golden wine seemed to lift us a finger's breadth above the turf and hold us suspended.[1]

The scene is from the 1981 television adaptation of Evelyn Waugh's *Brideshead Revisited*, and marks a moment of utter stillness and contentment for the two young men, one of whom will slide slowly into alcoholism, while the other attempts to find a place in a dysfunctional titled family that is collapsing in on itself during the inexorable march towards the Second World War.[2]

Sebastian and Charles's reverie underneath the oak tree is both enchanting and deeply tragic. Both have momentarily escaped university life at Oxford to take a country jaunt in a

A still from the television adaptation of *Brideshead Revisited*, 1981.

stolen car; a journey that will lead them to Flyte's ancestral home, Brideshead. Their brief picnic allows the young men to stop and be, lost in romantic dreams that the real world is soon to shatter. This is a moment of innocence and a wish for transcendence, and is one of the most memorable scenes from the series. The 1980s adaptation of *Brideshead Revisited* seemed to glory in the yearning for a more innocent conceptualization of Englishness, and as Charles and Sebastian lazed, one could almost imagine the gentle strains of Nick Drake's 'River Man' echoing the evocation of English pastoralism.[3] Drake's music seems to suggest a moment of stillness that is linked to rural bliss and a suspension between the mundane nature of reality and the potentiality of something far greater and unknowable. While Drake's music was never used for *Brideshead Revisited*, the picnic scene and 'River Man' seem to echo the same inherent Englishness: something that seems both timeless and deeply rooted in the past. They both convey an intangible quality that nonetheless speaks of a landscape that is instantly recognizable and deeply longed for.

This book is an attempt to understand why it may be possible to make that link, not only between one short scene in a 1980s television series and one short song in one artist's canon, but more broadly between much of Drake's music and the idea of Englishness. It is a connection made by many, as we shall see, and it is not simply to do with the fact of Drake's nationality. Nick Drake's music connects to deep sentiments that resonate with something indefinable yet deeply recognizable within the English psyche. It is a resonance that seems to extend beyond the boundaries of England itself, and goes some way to explain the enduring popularity of Drake's work far beyond his death in 1974.

This book is not a biography of Nick Drake – that has already been accomplished in two English-language works by Patrick Humphries and Trevor Dann, respectively, which paint an illuminating picture of the highly enigmatic musician.[4] However, for the purposes of the discussion to follow, it is worth sketching out Drake's life here. Nick Drake was born to Rodney and Molly Drake on 19 June 1948 in Rangoon, Burma.[5] Rodney worked for the Bombay Burmah Trading Corporation, commencing his employment in the 1930s as an engineer, and by 1940 he had become second in command at the Rangoon office of the BBTC. As the Second World War became more drawn out, Rodney was moved to Jhelum in what is now Pakistan. During this period, the Drakes' first child, Gabrielle, was born in 1944 in Lahore. By May 1945 Rodney, returned to Rangoon with his family to reconstruct the BBTC operation, but following Burmese independence in 1948, it became Rodney's job to oversee the transfer of the logging industry to the newly formed Burmese government. During this period, the couple's second child, Nicholas Rodney Drake, was born and with the winding up of the BBTC's operation in Burma, the Drake family relocated in 1952 to the hub of a rapidly disintegrating empire.

Upon the Drake family's return to Britain, they settled in the quiet Warwickshire village of Tanworth-in-Arden, a place that still seems to represent a quintessential ideal of English rural life. Rodney took up a position at Wolseley Engineering in Birmingham, a mere 15 miles away from the tranquillity of Tanworth, and soon rose to the positions of both chairman and managing director of the company. The Drakes lived an affluent upper-middle-class lifestyle in England with their Burmese Karen housekeeper Rosie, known to them as 'Nanny'.

Theirs was a family that fostered musical creativity, with a dedicated 'music room' in their home, Far Leys, where many of Nick's early demos were recorded, and the family would unite to perform informal recitals. Two of Molly Drake's own songs, 'Poor Mum' and 'Do You Ever Remember?', were released on the *Family Tree* compilation album in 2007, giving a sense of the musical lineage which must have been influential in some ways in his early years.

Nick attended preparatory school at Eagle House in the county of Berkshire, in southeast England, from 1957 until 1961, after which he was enrolled at Marlborough College, a private boarding school in Wiltshire in the southwest. Although a relatively skilled sportsman, Nick had a mixed academic record at Marlborough College and was required to return for a further year to retake his A-level examinations in 1965.

By December 1966, Nick had been offered a place at Fitzwilliam College at the University of Cambridge to read English. However, one requirement of entry was that he develop his French-language skills and to this end the Drakes funded a six-month trip to Aix-en-Provence near Marseilles. During this time, Drake continued to hone the musical skills that had first been fostered in the family home, where both Rodney and Molly were keen amateur musicians, and later at Marlborough, where he had played piano and saxophone. By the time Nick had moved to Aix with his friends Simon Crocker and Jeremy Mason, who were also studying at

Barton Hill dormitory, Nick's residence during his first year at Marlborough College, Wiltshire.

the university there, he was developing his guitar skills and busking around the area.

Drake returned to England and enrolled at Fitzwilliam College in 1967. While he never completed his degree, Cambridge acted as the crucible within which his musical career began. Most notably, it would lead to Drake's collaboration with a student called Robert Kirby, then attending Gonville and Caius College in the city, who would go on to provide orchestrations and arrangements for his first two albums. During the Cambridge years, Drake refined his musical style, became an accomplished guitarist and soon started playing gigs around the city and in London. It was while playing a benefit concert at the Roundhouse venue in Chalk Farm, Camden – supporting, amongst others, Country Joe and the Fish – that Drake was spotted by Ashley Hutchings, then bass player for the folk-rock act Fairport Convention. Hutchings introduced Drake to Joe Boyd, the music impresario and founder of the Witchseason production and management company. Boyd signed Drake and between 1969 and 1972 he made three albums for Witchseason: *Five Leaves Left, Bryter Layter* and *Pink Moon*.[6]

These three albums act as the core of the Drake mythos, and in many ways they chart three distinct periods in his life. *Five Leaves Left* collects a number of songs written at Tanworth, Aix and Cambridge, and was recorded and released while Drake was still continuing his studies at Fitzwilliam College. However, by the end of 1969, Drake had abandoned Cambridge and moved to London to concentrate on his musical career and therefore left his degree unfinished. His second album, *Bryter Layter*, is a more fully polished, pop-oriented product than its primarily acoustic predecessor, and is often considered his 'London' album. Despite relatively favourable reviews of both releases, Drake's music sold very poorly – a situation that seems to have frustrated him greatly. It was at this time that Drake, a somewhat shy and insular young man, started to exhibit signs of the depression and anxiety that would plague him for the rest of his life, and which were possibly aggravated by his well-documented and significant use of marijuana. Around this time he retreated from playing live altogether and lived a solitary existence in London, retreating from his friends and the music industry.

Drake's final album, *Pink Moon*, has been coloured retrospectively by the final years of his life. It certainly seems to mirror the singer's somewhat isolated existence, both in its arrangement (the entire album lasts a mere 29 minutes and consists only of Drake's voice and guitar with one piano overdub on the title track) and its lyrical preoccupations. The album was recorded without Boyd, who had acted as producer on the first two albums. By this time, Boyd had relocated to America to work for Warner Bros and Nick turned to John Wood, the engineer for *Five Leaves Left* and *Bryter Layter*, to produce the album. Again, the album did not sell well and for the next two years the disappointed singer would return to his family home in Tanworth-in-Arden and largely turn his back on the music industry. His mental health continued to deteriorate, and the period at Far Leys seems to have been an attempt to recuperate after the abortive London enterprise.

By early 1974 Nick Drake had decided that he wanted to return to the studio, and he joined Wood and Boyd to record a number of songs that would appear on his next album. Despite the fractious nature of his relationship with Boyd at this time, Drake seemed to be feeling more positive and his thoughts turned again to his own future. The situation changed dramatically on the morning of 25 November 1974, when Molly Drake entered her son's bedroom to find him lying lifeless on his bed. Nick had taken an overdose of the Tryptizol tablets that he had been prescribed for his depression. Whether he meant to kill himself is unclear and will probably never be known. Yet it is clear that on his death at the age of 26, Nick Drake's life and musical legacy were cut sadly short.

In many ways the story after Nick's death says much more about his status now than any specific aspects of his life. While Drake sold very few records in his lifetime, his posthumous popularity has grown unabated. Since the mid-1980s, a wealth of musicians have started to credit Drake as a formative influence on their work. My first engagement with Nick Drake was while listening to Julianne Regan, then singer with the British band All About Eve, talking about him while being interviewed on BBC Radio 1 in 1988. It was during this broadcast that I first heard 'River Man' and my own fascination with Drake commenced. Artists such as Paul Weller, Beck, The Cure, REM and Badly Drawn Boy have all championed Drake's music, and following the use of the song 'Pink Moon' in a television advertisement for the Volkswagen Cabriolet in 1999, Drake's albums sold more in one month than during his entire lifetime.

Three documentary films have been made about Drake: *A Stranger Among Us – In Search of Nick Drake*, *A Skin too Few: The Days of Nick Drake* and *Nick Drake: Under Review*.[7] Similarly, a number of radio documentaries, including *Lost Boy: In Search of Nick Drake*, narrated by Brad Pitt for BBC Radio 2, have opened his music up to a wider audience.[8] Alongside the use of his music in adverts, television programmes and films, several books, most notably Humphries's and Dann's offerings, have chronicled his life. In 2007 Amanda Petrusich published a book on *Pink Moon* as part of Continuum's *33 ⅓* series on classic albums.[9] In 2009 Omnibus Press published *Nick Drake: The Complete Guide to his Music*.[10] More recently, Jason Creed published *Nick Drake: The Pink Moon Files*, a collection of articles reprinted from his *Pynk Moon* fanzine dedicated to Nick, shedding further light on the enigmatic singer.[11] At the time of writing, the manager of Drake's estate, Cally Callomon, is putting together a book of unreleased letters, photographs and other material from the Drake family archive, and further books will no doubt follow.

Just prior to his own death in 2008, also from an overdose of antidepressants, the actor Heath Ledger had talked about his ambition to bring a biopic of Drake to fruition, while in 2010, a short tour of tribute concerts curated by Joe Boyd toured the UK, featuring artists such as Teddy Thompson, Green Gartside, Robyn Hitchcock and Vashti Bunyan performing Drake's songs. The tour's performance was broadcast on BBC Four in the UK and was followed, as part of the channel's Nick Drake Night, by *A Skin Too Few*.[12] In addition to such obvious signs of Drake's work seeping into the wider culture, there have been several releases – a box set of his albums, as well as a number of compilations and albums of unreleased material – all of which adds to the Drake story. His followers from all over the world continue to celebrate his life at annual musical gatherings at the Church of St Mary Magdalene in Tanworth, where he is buried, and the family grave continues to be a site of pilgrimage for the Drake faithful. Drake, like Charles and Sebastian, now rests beneath an oak tree overlooking the bucolic Warwickshire countryside.

Why has Nick Drake become so significant after his death when his music passed largely unnoticed during his lifetime? This book is an attempt to understand, if not the totality of Drake's appeal globally, then one part of his representation that seems significant to his enduring appeal. Nick Drake has become synonymous with a certain image of English national identity, an image that seems often contradictory and nostalgic, yet one which continues to resonate some four decades after his death. This image (by which I mean not only his visual iconography but the entire phenomenon, incorporating music, imagery, biography and subsequent mythology) is nicely summed up by an email posted on the website of the musician Keith James, who regularly performs concerts of Drake's music to audiences who perhaps never had the chance to see him live. Following one concert at the Millfield Theatre in North London in 2006, a member of the audience (who only gives his name as 'Robert') sent the following message to James to reflect upon the night and Drake himself:

> My own experience of Nick Drake's music was at a boarding school not too dissimilar to Marlborough (Worcester in fact) with *Five Leaves Left* playing on the little hi-fi in the study. The end of the summer term looking out across College Green in the Dean's close on the private side of the cathedral. Verdant green with the dulcet tones musing over the lawns under the wide spreading trees. Nick fitted so well into that privileged time. Choristers, dope and Englishness. That was 1974, and I didn't even know that he was dead. We lived in a small village outside Stratford-[up]on-Avon (Alveston) and various '-in-Arden' places were close by. I had never strayed as close to Brum [Birmingham] as Ta[n]worth but was not surprised by what I saw when I dropped by recently. Upper-middle class dormitory postcards for the conurbation. It must have been with very mixed emotions when he returned home after his 'triumph' in

London. The one image that does stick in my head from after
I discovered the full story of his life and death is him driving
his mum's Mini without direction or reason until he ran out
of petrol then phoned home unable to say where he was.[13]

Robert's recollections mark out some significant themes
that seem to recur throughout people's reactions to Drake's
work: on the one hand, the privilege of a private education
and dreamlike meditations on the English landscape, and on
the other, the complex of picturesque rurality and urban
modernity that situate Drake's music both temporally and
spatially. However, Drake's meanderings, not only journeys
that took place as aimless drives in the last few years of his life
but his nomadic existence in London and more generally,
perhaps, a sense of rootlessness that goes back to his first years
in Burma, give a sense of someone adrift and wandering. The
use of the words 'search' and 'lost' among responses to Drake's
work after his death mark out not only his mental dislocation
from the world but also his significance as a cipher through
which we may understand Englishness as a quality that is as
absent or elusive as it is present.

Yet it is the 'choristers [and] dope' image that most perfectly
sums up Drake's significance. Drake stands historically between
a vision of England that is steeped in the Anglican tradition and
rural nostalgia and a moment of modernity influenced as much
by North America and Europe as it is by anything specifically
English. Nick Drake's music, while often alluringly unspecific (itself a characteristic that may account for its enduring attraction),
provides a possibility of conciliation between a view of Englishness that looks back to a Romantic ideal of the pastoral while
also situating itself within a Britain that was changing rapidly in
the post-war years. These years remade the national landscape –
not only physically but socially, culturally and intellectually.

That Drake is often described as an 'English' artist rather than a British one, noticeably in England itself, suggests a certain form of national identity that is not inclusive, not applicable to all, in a country that is now more culturally and ethnically diverse than it was during Drake's own lifetime. Yet he does present us with a way of thinking about England and Englishness that seems *of use* now. While Drake's music never engages with national identity in an overt sense, part of his appeal after his death has been fostered by the use of his music in certain contexts, particularly film and television. These uses have often placed Drake's acoustic music as pastoral soundtrack, rooting his music in contexts that, whether they might have been intended by Drake or not, have gone a long way to shaping perceptions of him and his music.

The following chapters seek to map out the territory of Drake's significance as a musical icon of Englishness. His is not the only version of Englishness in popular music that one might point to, and indeed, as suggested above, he certainly does not represent the totality of English national experience, even at certain times in the country's history. But one must ask why Drake specifically is so often associated with the idea of Englishness when other comparable musicians might not be. This connection says a lot more about Drake's musical legacy and the uses of his music after his death than it does about the small body of work that he leaves behind. Yet the intertwined story of his musical output and his biography have ramifications for the version of Englishness that he seems to represent, the choristers and dope, the whimsical nostalgia and the existential bohemianism.

What follows marks out the territory within which notions of Englishness may be understood and the influences that inform Drake's music as well as the reception of it, both during his lifetime and subsequently. This is a particular manifestation of Englishness that speaks of the relationship between the urban and the rural, one that draws on the rhythms and timbres of the English landscape and a progressive tendency manifested through the formative British counterculture in the 1960s. This is an articulation of Englishness that circles around introspection and melancholia, rootlessness and wandering, and it is finally a manifestation of Englishness that continues to present itself not only in the uses of Drake's music and legacy but in comparative strains of popular music by other singularly 'English' artists. Above all, this book asks why Nick Drake as an artist and the music that he made may be useful to summon up a vision of a certain national identity, particularly long after that artist has ceased to be materially part of that nation. In this sense this book is not about Nick Drake's music as much as it is about how we understand England through what he left behind.

1 DREAMING ENGLAND

There are no explicit references to England, the country, or indeed Britain, the political union, anywhere in the music of Nick Drake. Drake's music certainly cannot be said to be overtly patriotic, or even overly specific about place in any way, aside from a few cursory references to London, and his lyrics fail to engage with any sense of an English people, or a national identity, in any meaningful manner.[1] However, particularly since his death, Drake has often been placed within a context that situates him and his music as specifically English. While such claims are often rather vaguely put, others seek to situate Drake within a specifically English musical or lyrical tradition. Whatever claims are made about Drake's work (and Drake made precious few claims about his own work, granting only one interview with Jerry Gilbert to *Sounds* magazine in March 1971 that constitutes only 236 words from the interviewee with no detail about his music or lyrics whatsoever) they are made from outside; that is to say, from his audience – an audience that is very much of the present. As such, they say more about how people find a way to express Englishness through his music than about how his music says anything about Englishness.

Clearly, however, there must be some locus, some point of contact, that causes such claims to be made. I will return to Drake's music and lyrical preoccupations in more detail, factors that point towards potentially English (and international) characteristics, but first some clarification of what Englishness stands for. Englishness, as with most conceptions of national identity, is a particularly difficult idea to define. On a broad level one may choose to define Englishness as a set of characteristics ascribed to or exemplified by the people that inhabit or originate from the geographical space that is England. Yet what seems most immediately apparent when listening to Nick Drake's music is that it can only be said to articulate specific states of Englishness; it does not – and perhaps cannot – connect with the multiplicity of experience that constitutes England as a totality at any given time, past or present. Therefore the associations we make between Nick Drake's music and Englishness say much about how that very concept may be understood within certain contexts, even if they fail to account for English perspectives that step outside Drake's frame of reference. Nick Drake's music may say little to people about contemporary England – of working-class life or of the post-immigrant experience, for example – yet the very fact that his music is often utilized to represent what Englishness may mean points to certain ways of thinking about national identity in England, even at the start of the twenty-first century.

Before thinking about what constitutes national identity, or more specifically Englishness, the claims made about Drake's work provide a useful starting point. Whenever Nick Drake is mentioned in relation to Englishness, two broad themes emerge. The first of these themes concerns the Englishness of Drake's music specifically. This theme can be further divided into two strains: Drake's music as it sits within a repertoire of English music, and as it seems to exhibit specifically English musical characteristics. The first strain places little judgement upon the music or lyrics themselves and is more concerned with Nick Drake's music within a temporal and spatial context. Ian MacDonald, writing in *Mojo* magazine in 2000, suggests that 'River Man' is 'the centrepiece of Drake's early period, both artistically and in terms of his personal outlook, [it] is one of the sky-high classics of post-war English popular music'.[2] Len Brown, writing in *New Musical Express* (NME) in 1986, voices a similar sentiment when he describes 'Northern Sky' from *Bryter Layter* as 'the greatest English love song of modern times'.[3] Both claims seem to work on two levels. They both situate specific songs within a body of work that extends beyond Drake and that may include other artists, but is bounded spatially (music originating from English musicians) and temporally ('post-war' and 'modern times', while somewhat vague, give a sense of a frame within which such claims might be understood).

Yet both views hint at another level of meaning that extends beyond when and where the music was released. Both MacDonald and Brown seem to hint not only at the fact of Drake's music being constituted within an English temporal and spatial context but at the quality of that music connecting to something more oblique and abstract. In an article for the *Sunday Telegraph* in 1997, Mick Brown suggests that in an age when

> the prevalent musical influences were American, Drake's music had an unmistakably English quality. His songs, melodies and open-tuned guitar playing owed as much to his love of Vaughan Williams and Delius as to Dylan and the Band; his lyrics were as much influenced by the vernacular and sensibility of the 19th-century Romantic poets, as by the locutions of blues and folk, lending his themes of love, yearning and self-identity a particular literacy.[4]

The strap line of the article accentuates this point by describing Drake as 'a very English singer'. Here the subtexts that may be read into MacDonald's and Brown's claims are made evident as Drake's music and lyrics are understood to connect to specific strains of culture associated with England and Englishness.

These kinds of claims are frequently made in descriptions of Drake's work, and they connect with differing aspects of what his music provides. One common connection is made through the quality of Drake's singing voice and his vocal delivery. Among the promotional material advertising a Drake tribute concert at the Barbican in London in September 1999 (part of a series of concerts branded *English Originals*) is his music, exemplified by 'his intricate guitar work, introspective songs and understated English voice'.[5] The musician Paul Thompson echoes Mick Brown when he says, 'I like the Englishness of [Drake's] pronunciation at a time when many British artists were trying to sound as American as possible.'[6] Clearly the manner in which Drake delivers his lines suggests a certain national character that is easy to identify.

More frequent than claims about Drake's voice are claims about his music's relationship to Englishness or English musical traditions. Sometimes these claims are very specific; sometimes they are more vague. In another article from *Mojo*, Mark Cooper describes 'Drake's peculiarly English chamber music'.[7] Another, posted on the website of music magazine *Magnet*, describes the song 'Northern Sky' as 'unfussy English pop'.[8] Both of these observations highlight potential musical genres or styles that we may connect Drake's music with. Again there is a sense of geographical boundaries but the respective time frames differ, pointing to contrasting stylistic elements within Drake's music. Thus his music, at least in light of the two views above, is both 'chamber music' – a point most evident in tracks such as 'Way to Blue' or 'Fruit Tree' – and 'pop music'. The use of the term 'unfussy' seems to set this particular version of pop music apart, presumably most significantly from any Americanized versions of that form. It may be pop, but it is restrained, uncluttered and not histrionic. Whether this is true or not, and whether non-English popular music may be said to hold contrary values or not, something is being suggested about what English pop music might be before any engagement with Drake's music takes place. As such, both perspectives offer up a space that exists prior to Drake that his work can be understood to sit within.

Two musical contemporaries of Drake's, John Martyn and Vashti Bunyan, have also commented upon the 'Englishness' of Drake's music. Bunyan, talking ahead of another Drake tribute show in Brighton in 2010, said: 'Nick Drake and I were siblings in Joe Boyd's family. I think Joe, coming from America, appreciated the innate Englishness of our music in a way nobody here could see.'[9] Martyn, a close personal friend of Drake, suggested to Richard Skinner in an interview broadcast on BBC Radio 1 in 1986 that 'it's just very good music. It's very British isn't it? And that's one of the things I like about it.'[10] Martyn goes on to situate Drake's 'Britishness' in opposition again to American influences, but both Bunyan's and Martyn's perceptions underplay the complex web of influences and stylistic associations evident in Drake's work that extend across England and Britain's national borders. Chris Jones, in a review of *Five Leaves Left*, gets closer when he describes Drake's music as 'a whole different kettle of Englishness, with more than a hint of jazz about it'.[11] Clearly the status of Drake's Englishness is more complex than Bunyan and Martyn suggest and it is a subject that we will return to.

I suggested earlier in this chapter that there were two themes that were often used to connect Nick Drake to concepts of English national identity. While the first is most audible in his music and lyrics, as we have seen above, the second of these themes is potentially more abstract, as it often seems to exist above or outside Nick Drake's recorded output. Here connections are made to Englishness via a further two strains: landscape and psychology. While both might be articulated through Drake's music, there is a wider sense of Drake's internal and external environment that audiences might relate to.

Drake's connection to landscape and environment seems strange, given the lack of specificity of place in his lyrics, yet as we shall see in the next chapter, they are significant themes not only in his lyrics but in people's responses to his music. Ian MacDonald paints a vivid picture of place in his writing on Drake's music:

> To listen to Nick Drake is to step out of this world of pose and noise, and enter a quiet, oak-panelled room, dappled with sun-light – a room opening, through French windows, into a lush green garden, equally quiet because we're in the country, far from the sound of the city. It's summer, bees and birds are abroad in the shade, and, beyond the nearby trees, a soft tangle of voices and convivial laughter can be felt, along with the dipping of languid oars in a rushy river that winds through cool woods and teeming meadows hereabouts: an English landscape with Gallic ghosts from *Le Grand Meaulnes* and *La maison de Claudine*. And an acoustic guitar playing gently beyond the hedgerow in jazzy 5/4.[12]

Here Drake is playing in the open air, unseen within an intrinsically English landscape. But of course there is more at play here – European and American voices, we note, come together in the English garden, much as they do within Drake's music. The British musician Alison Goldfrapp has made of connections:

> I think also what I like about Nick Drake is that he makes me think of England, you know? English countryside, ruralness – which a lot of folk music does . . . There's not that much English folk music that is really appealing. But with Nick Drake there's so much atmosphere to it, which is why so many people like it.[13]

Jonathan Wolff, writing in Jason Creed's *Pynk Moon* fanzine, works the other way around. Wolff is recounting a trip to

Nick's family grave at St Mary Magdalene, Tanworth-in-Arden.

Tanworth-in-Arden to visit Drake's grave, followed by a visit to nearby Stratford-upon-Avon to see a production of *Romeo and Juliet*. He describes his day as 'all very autumnal, very English, very Nick Drake'.[14] Here, Drake becomes the yardstick by which to measure environment, whereas MacDonald approaches the relationship from the other direction. It is interesting to note that the two writers associate Drake's music with different seasons, although the connection to autumn suggests a specific interiorized state that forms the second strain of relationships between Drake and Englishness.

Perhaps because of his death at a very young age, possibly by his own hand, much has been made of Drake's mental state and a perceived melancholy within his music. This sense of melancholy (perhaps evident in Wolff's association of Drake's music with autumn rather than summer) is often used in the discourse around him to signal a national trait, or at least an English response to the world. Len Brown describes *Five Leaves Left* as 'a masterpiece of

English melancholy', while Mark Cooper evaluates his music as 'a continuous stream of melancholic contemplation'.[15] Barney Hoskyns, reviewing the *Family Tree* compilation of Drake's early recordings in *Uncut* magazine, makes similar statements.[16] Hoskyns suggests that:

> There's a peculiarly English bashfulness to Drake that suggests some coy conflation of Donovan and Colin Blunstone. Listen with both ears and you hear the monkish beauty of that light baritone alongside its close companion – Drake's inimitably intricate fingerpicking. Together these intertwined "voices" create a melancholic magic that sounds completely unique to this day.[17]

Here Hoskyns is touching on a number of characteristics that situate Drake's music as English: a particularly English kind of shyness or reserve; a simple, austere aesthetic; and again, melancholy. Of course, what such perceptions reveal, above and beyond Drake's music, is how we all might imagine Englishness, using Nick Drake to do so.

Clearly, the writers mentioned above are responding to Nick Drake's music in ways that sketch out the terrain (at least for them) of Englishness, but outside Drake's work the concept of nationhood and national identity requires further interrogation if it is to work in any meaningful sense. Nations, nation-states (independent states with some level of ethnic, cultural or linguistic homogeneity) and nation states (states that may be held together by a collective sense of civic identity) may all be bounded geographically, yet their borders or limits in space tell us little about how the inhabitants of such places understand their own sense of a collective national self.[18] Indeed, even geographical boundaries change over time, and England's shifting relationship with its neighbours, Wales, Scotland and Northern Ireland, has produced a dynamic set of national and regional identities refracted through ideas of Britishness.

National identity itself is even more dynamic and porous, fluctuating over time and in relation to internal and external influences. Whenever I ask my undergraduate students how important a sense of national identity is to them, few express any real connection to Englishness, Britishness or whatever national identity they may potentially identify with. Some express a deeper connection to 'regionality' (particularly those from the north of England, often centred around northeast and northwest regional identification), but national identity only seems to come to the fore in one of two circumstances: moments of collective national endeavour, particularly sporting events, and when travelling abroad. This latter manifestation of national consciousness seems to either take the form of embarrassment at the actions of other English travellers, or of a sense of representing one's nation abroad in a positive manner.

What both responses show is that national identity is often constituted in relation to an 'other', be it another football team or a foreign country and its people. Ernest Renan's claim that 'unity is always effected by means of brutality', while stressing the way in which a sense of nationhood is fostered by violence – whether through invasion, insurrection or rebellion – points to the way in which national identity acts as a means to collectively identify a group in the face of opposition.[19] In this sense it becomes harder to talk about national identity as a 'thing' in and of itself; rather, national identity becomes an effect of discourse and dialogue between elements. As such, we encounter two main problems in our attempt to understand Drake in relation to any specific sense of national identity. The first problem concerns any attempt to homogenize a populace under an umbrella of a specific national identity, while the second concerns the ways in which Drake's music shapes that notion of national identity.

The first issue might be usefully dealt with by defining exactly what we may mean by national identity. David Miller suggests that the role of the nation is to foster a sense of collective civic identity that replicates relationships found at a more local level. In this way, large, anonymous nation states are able to foster a sense of collective identity that might allow them to function. Miller suggests five characteristics that limit or define national identity: a set of shared beliefs; a sense of historical continuity; opportunities for the nation to indulge in collective action or events; a link to a specific geographical space; and a common set of characteristics (over and above demarcations of ethnicity or religion, for example).[20] One could also stress the importance of a political community with common institutions and a code of rights and duties shared by that community, bounded both geographically and by a sense of belonging.[21]

Such attempts to understand what national identity could be stress the tension or relationship between the actions that people are involved in as part of a nation and the institutions that might shape that nation materially. England is a case in point here, as its relationships with the other parts of the UK have altered in recent years through increased levels of devolution. This process has brought with it a renewed sense of England as a state in some ways increasingly apart from its immediate neighbours, and this has been reflected in a growing interest, at least in terms of musical culture, in music that seems to engage with English folk identity both past and present.[22] In this way, national identity becomes a dynamic process, constantly redefining itself in relation to (often) outside influences. However, whether an entire national populace understands itself through that identity, or even a range of identities within a national corpus, is more problematic.

I said above that there was a second issue to engage with here, and that is how culture, and more specifically the music of Nick Drake, engages with the material reality of a geographically and

politically defined nationhood. One of the most influential
discussions of national identity in recent years comes from
Benedict Anderson's *Imagined Communities* – a text that continues
to have ramifications for the study of nation and nationalism
even twenty years after its revised edition. Inevitably, Anderson
also attempts to define the nation as something more elusive
and incorporeal:

> I propose the following definition of the nation: it is an
> imagined political community – and imagined as both
> inherently limited and sovereign. It is *imagined* because
> the members of even the smallest nation will never
> know most of their fellow-members, meet them, or
> even hear of them, yet in the minds of each lives the
> image of their communion.[23]

While the nation may be limited geographically, even if such a
boundary is in flux, and it may be sovereign in its independence,
its means of understanding itself are idealized. Anderson is keen
to note that this imaginary status does not mean that it is false or
fictitious; rather, the process of collective imagination itself
constitutes national identity. In this way, national identity is by
definition ambivalent, an imaginary field that is in a constant state
of becoming, never fully realized or concretized.[24] The implication
of this is that rather than finding national identity in the monolithic
institutions of any given country, it can be felt in the oscillations
between a country's own changing view of itself and its similarly
changing view of the outside world.

The very concept of 'the nation' has been largely eclipsed in
recent years by studies of the local and the global.[25] Where it is
highlighted, the nation, particularly within studies of popular music,
tends to be understood either as a historical relic, a marketing
mechanism or a site of defence against globalization. What such

approaches fail to offer is a route by which popular music may constitute or contribute to the ambivalent imagining of national identity. Music's role in relation to national identity is often as a means to 'reterritorialize', to contribute to the ambivalent dialogue, in a liminal interspace that connects both to local specificity and to global flows of economic and cultural capital.

In this conceptual space the perceptions of Drake's Englishness that we encountered earlier assume significance not because they may be right or wrong, but because they constitute how Nick Drake's music is used to imagine English national identity. They have, of course, been chosen because they reference Englishness in relation to Nick Drake, and many thousands of words have been written on Drake without recourse to positioning him as an archetype of Englishness. Yet the consistent implication by many that there is a connection suggests that Drake's music, already ambivalent in many ways, as we shall see, provides a space to contest and construct Englishness in certain ways. Sometimes these claims are made in connection to perceived English characteristics in existence prior to Drake's music (or even potentially emergent after his death), and as such, it is worth considering how English national identity has been 'imagined' through its art and culture.

Menno Spiering, in his meditation on post-war English literature, comments that 'national identity, and by implication English identity, is what people feel it to be':

> National identity is an image, it carries meaning in the sense that it abides in feelings and convictions; often it is part and parcel of an ideology. Hence the images can be examined in as far as they are expressed in, for instance, documents, but that is the limit of any objective, scholarly approach to the matter. The images may be collected and sorted, or their origins, development and functions in time may be traced,

or in a more literary-theoretic approach their textual or
intertextual usages may be analysed. No pronouncement,
however, can be made about their 'justness.'[26]

Certainly, if we are to understand English national identity as an
imaginary category, as something which acts not only at a collective
level but also in a multiplicity of ways at individual levels, then the
task of defining what Englishness may be becomes almost impossible. Yet the imagination of Englishness must be constituted
through practices such as politics, legislature and, of course, culture.
As Philip V. Bohlman observes, the links between music and
nationalism were forged during the post-Enlightenment period as
a means of articulating a unified national consciousness.[27] One of
the means of achieving this was through the organization of
regional folk musics into a national repertoire, a canon of music
representative of a national identity even as, through the twentieth
century, such musics assumed the ability to transcend national
borders through emergent media, such as the radio. Here, music
becomes subsumed into a general national publicity, where a
populace 'experiences' its own identity through listening to music
broadcast over national networks.[28] As such, music becomes a
means to mark out a space of Englishness that people may use
to imagine themselves in certain ways.

This relationship between national character and culture is
outlined by the German-born art historian Nikolaus Pevsner in
The Englishness of English Art, written in 1956.[29] This relationship
makes pronouncements on the 'justness' or value of art both
through the way in which it may represent a sense of national
identity, and through the way in which it may transcend insularity
or isolationism. For Pevsner, the most valuable works of art are
those which are highly expressive of national character while at
the same time being conscious of their own historicity, and so
provide a context for national sentiment that evades jingoism.[30]

Pevsner was aware of a tension between how a nation might understand itself, as expressed through art and culture, and nationalism as a force with a potentially regressive or outright violent outcome. Thus national identity as it is expressed through art is of value when it expresses the dynamic tension between past and present, inside and outside.

Under Pevsner's criteria, Nick Drake's music comes into focus in a particular way. As we shall see in subsequent chapters, Drake's songs, often erroneously framed as 'folk' music, and certainly attached to the English landscape, manage both a connection to strains of English tradition and nostalgia, and an utterly contemporary engagement with both non-English musical forms and a series of historical tensions inherent in what Drake represents.[31] He is 'of value' because he represents a point of articulation or ambivalence between England and its 'others' that works to shape Englishness itself.

England has consistently evaded national definition, subsuming itself within other political identities such as Great Britain, the United Kingdom or the British Empire.[32] However, three broad themes emerge from national discourse that provide often competing visions of Englishness and what it might mean. These themes might be described as conservatism, conciliation and confrontation. The conservative (not to be explicitly linked to the British Conservative Party, or indeed a necessarily and particular right-wing conservative political ideology) prism might broadly be understood as a means of rediscovering a sense of English identity, as something that has been lost. Here, Englishness is largely constituted as defensive: a defence against the encroachment of modernity, immigration, European and American integration, the mass media, socialism and a myriad of other 'ills'. It is this approach to Englishness that lays the strongest claim to connections to landscape and nostalgia, both significant features in people's responses to the work of Nick Drake. Here England is lost, often to be rediscovered in some prelapsarian quasi-feudal or pastoral imagined past.

The magazine *This England*, which since its first issue in 1986 has sought to cement an image of England that is often rural and oriented around the countryside and the village, proposes a set of 'timeless English values' that may provide a defence against a perceived embattled national identity.[33] Despite a stated intention to remain largely apolitical in the first few issues, the magazine has increasingly espoused a neoconservative political stance that understands England and Englishness as under attack. The editor, Stephen Garnett, provides more than a hint of such defensiveness when writing about youth crime in his 'Editor's Letter':

> The breakdown of family life, an absence of discipline in the home and at school, exposure to violent computer games and television programmes, the lack of a proper education, the moral bankruptcy of certain sections of society . . . these and numerous other reasons have been given to explain the worrying surge in violence. I suspect it is a poisonous cocktail of them all . . . The readers of *This England* are the eyes and ears of England, the people on the front line.[34]

Garnett's indignation coupled with the clarion call to the nation's defence sits alongside articles on the historic homes of England, its literary landscapes (in this particular issue, quoted above, it concentrates on the inspiration for Richard Adams's novel *Watership Down* of 1972), William the Conqueror and tea made by PG Tips. While much of *This England* seems relatively benign in its evocation of a rural England under threat from the ravages of modernity and liberalism, it marks the more palatable end of a spectrum that includes extremist national political movements such as the British National Party. Featherstone points to Simon Heffer and Roger Scruton as recent commentators on

Englishness who have espoused a similar re-engagement with mythic forms of Englishness to challenge the perceived disappearance of a national culture, particularly as the devolutionary process atomizes the United Kingdom.[35]

The idea that England might be a lost country, something to be regained, is central to Rob Young's *Electric Eden*.[36] Young shows how folk traditions have been consistently used within much English (and British) popular music to engage with a mythic or visionary past, often framed as Albion, in the face of modernity. While such strategies may be understood to be nostalgic revisionism, potentially associated with a conservative political ideology despite bohemian pretensions, they perhaps highlight instead not so much what is being sought as what prompts such seeking. English identity may also be understood through a process of conciliation: a dialogue between an imagined past, often highly pastoral in nature, and an increasingly internationalist and industrialized present. In popular music, folk rock, with its recourse not only to English (and other) folk forms but also to American rock 'n' roll and amplified instrumentation, provides an example of such conciliation.

The consistent model for such conciliation in relation to English national identity is George Orwell. Featherstone suggests that:

> Nearly sixty years after his death in 1950, theorists of Englishness (and Britishness – Orwell never made much of a distinction), including Prime Ministers of the Right and the Left (John Major most famously, Gordon Brown most recently), have continued to use his essays as points of reference and authority. This is because Orwell offers a definition of England that mixes populism, patriotism and radicalism in a convincing voice and a supple syntax. His is an Englishness in discursive

The site of Nick's last photo-shoot with Keith Morris in 1971, Hampstead Ponds, London.

political motion, providing perspectives that can be applied
equally to common-sense Labourism, nostalgic Conservatism,
cautious Liberalism, anti-Americanism and Euro-scepticism.
His work remains an improbably useful resource for a nation
that still finds it hard to say exactly what it is.[37]

Orwell offers a vision of English patriotism that resists provincialism
and engages with a tradition of English radicalism that stretches
from peasant uprisings in the Middle Ages to contemporary
socialists and anarchists. Orwell's own socialism engages with
English national identity in his works 'The Lion and the Unicorn'
and *The English People*, largely as a response to the rise of fascism
both at home and abroad.[38] In this way, Englishness becomes
wrested from reactionary nationalism to become something that
connects to a particular English character with an eye for internationalism and democratic socialism. Orwell evokes green fields as
well as smoky towns, the modernity of the nineteenth century
firmly settled in among England's own traditions and settings.[39]
His vision of Englishness is an ambivalent one, characterized
by common sense, idiosyncrasy, anti-authoritarianism, fairness
and a sense of inarticulate patriotism. It is above all an attempt
at conciliation between competing visions of England, even
though it might at times seem contradictory.

At the beginning of the story of Nick Drake is empire. Drake's
birth in Rangoon and his father's employment in Burma mark the
final years of any meaningful British Empire, and it is significant
that Rodney Drake played an important role in handing over the
Bombay Burmah Trading Corporation to the newly formed
independent government. While the body of critical theory
surrounding the postcolonial experience has tended to focus
on countries both during colonization and after independence
and subsequent diasporas and emigrations to ex-colonial powers,
little focus has been paid to the experience of British expats as

they returned to their 'home land'. The relocation to the heart of a crumbling empire and a Britain irrevocably changed by the Second World War was very far from a homecoming, and for many it marked a significant change in social status, work practices and one's relationship to national identity. Indeed, it is significant how such repatriations would reshape the very nature of Englishness. The Drake family was emblematic of such an experience, finding itself, after almost twenty years away from the centre of empire, suddenly back deep within the heart of England. Their experience was not wholly unusual: George Orwell served as a policeman in Burma between 1922 and 1927 (although he returned to England voluntarily) and the writer J. G. Ballard, having lived in Shanghai for the first sixteen years of his life, repatriated following incarceration by invading Japanese forces during the Second World War.

The return to the roots of empire exhibits a tension between Britain as the 'homeland' (and England within it) and those who orchestrated that empire as expatriates. The Drake family, while often situated as the embodiment of upper-middle-class English respectability, returned from Burma as strangers. That is not to say that they were estranged from any sense of English identity, rather that the postcolonial experience marks a point of mutation. In this way, the experience of empire is significant not only in changing the identity of the colonized, but the colonizers. As the Drakes returned home, settling in the heart of the Warwickshire countryside acted as a means of integrating into what was ostensibly another foreign country. Paul Gilroy suggests that Britain's inability to mourn the loss of empire has resulted in a form of post-imperial melancholia that has led to the return of a mythologized past for England that is silent about its racial exclusivity.[40] This may account for Drake's work being situated so centrally within rural visions of England or Albion, particularly as Britain becomes a far less significant actor on the world stage after empire. In using Nick Drake to say something about Englishness, his internationalism has been relegated in favour of the more mythic themes of Englishness that might mark out an introverted and isolationist vision of national character. Yet such an understanding ignores other more progressive tendencies that could be found in his work.

The extent to which such dislocation consciously affected the four-year-old Nick Drake is questionable, but the tensions outlined above, between pastoral nostalgic revisionism, progressive politics and the hangover from the loss of empire, all find places within the legacy of his work and life. The next chapter considers Drake's music, its influences and its reception as they engage with conceptions of England that, while potentially contradictory, may find resolution or conciliation as they are focused through his songs.

2 LISTENING TO THE LAND

The writer and journalist Caitlin Moran makes explicit links between the music of Nick Drake and the English countryside when she describes the situation of his grave in the churchyard of St Mary Magdalene, Tanworth-in-Arden:

> You see the countryside, there's never anyone there. It's not like when you go to Jim Morrison's grave and it's covered in graffiti and kind of really skanky looking people are sort of hanging around with a kind of 'I told you so' look on their face. Everybody who goes to Nick Drake's grave has left an acorn, or a tiny bracelet or something. So what you notice is the countryside and you just think, yeah, this actually does make sense. This is what he wrote about, there aren't any people there for a reason. He wrote about this countryside. He wrote about, you know, the earth, he wrote about England, an imagined England, rather than people or places or times.[1]

The lack of specificity in Drake's work might make such a claim difficult to substantiate. There are many references and allusions to elements of the English landscape in the words of these songs, even if they might not be tied to specific places. Yet the feeling that his music in some ways evokes space, place and situation is strong and is a recurrent feature of people's reactions to his records. If Drake's elusive lyrics only hint at place, then how might we come to understand the ways in which such responses are formed? The answer lies, at least in part, in the sound of his music: the timbre and texture of the instrumentation, the relationships between instrumental voices and the evocation of space and time via rhythm and pitch. The first confrontation with Drake's land-scapes occurs via the sound of the music itself, and over the course of his three studio albums a variety of spaces, some benign, others more malignant, emerge to set the scene for his lyrics.

That such spaces could be considered quintessentially English suggests that the evocation of elemental spaces through the sound of his music is further connected to other factors that give it context. Three features – Drake's voice, the iconography surrounding his music and his biography – all help to determine the way in which the sounds that one hears when listening to his records may be understood before any particular analysis of his words might take place.[2]

It is interesting to note that most of the positioning of Drake's music as being particularly English has occurred since his death; something which is partly attributable to his cult status. One of the first things that most writers commenting on Nick Drake mention is that his three albums, *Five Leaves Left*, *Bryter Layter* and *Pink Moon*, all sold very poorly during his lifetime. Estimates vary, but Martin 'Cally' Callomon, who currently manages the singer's estate, suggests that:

> We can only guess as to how many albums Nick sold through Island up until 1988 as chart-monitoring and sales accounting changed through various systems over those 20 years and sales history was never carried forward. Suffice to say that anyone at Island would say that Nick sold NO records whilst he was with them. That is, his sales were on a par with Mick Abrahams, Claire Hamill, Jess Roden, and many other such Island acts, 3,000 per title would have been about right, 500 of which

The Warwickshire countryside seen from the churchyard at St Mary Magdalene, Tanworth-in-Arden.

would have disappeared as promo copies. Note that these are per-title. I know of a couple of people who bought all three albums, I suspect many did, so Nick's contemporary fan-base could have been as low as 1,000 people.[3]

Whatever the truth may be, Drake's music clearly had little significant impact when it was initially released. Most of these sales would have been domestic, and Drake had little more luck abroad.

Commentators usually follow up this evaluation of Drake's sales figures with what appears to be a contradictory judgement from music critics of the day. The mythology surrounding Drake suggests that while his music passed by the majority of the public (presumably due to a general lack of airplay and public appearances), his records were lauded by the music press. This claim tends to overemphasize the generosity of the reviews that Drake's music received. In fact, most reviews of his albums, while usually favourable, are often marked by a sense of bewilderment or frustration. An unnamed writer in *Melody Maker* had this to say about *Five Leaves Left*:

> All smokers will recognise the meaning of the title – it refers to the five leaves left near the end of a packet of cigarette papers. It sounds poetic and so does the composer, singer and guitarist Nick Drake. His debut album for Island is interesting.[4]

That brief response amounts to the entire sum of the writer's praise for the album. Jerry Gilbert's review of *Bryter Layter* in *Sounds* focuses on the support given to Drake by the producer and supporting musicians:

> I get the feeling that only a Joe Boyd – Paul Harris [pianist on *Bryter Layter*] alliance could have produced such a superb album as this. And once again a great slice of credit must go to Robert Kirby, whose splendid arrangements are as noticeable as they were on Nick Drake's last album.
>
> On their own merits, the songs of Nick Drake are not particularly strong, but Nick has always been a consistent if introverted performer, and placed in the cauldron that Joe Boyd has prepared for him, then things start to effervesce.[5]

Andrew Means for *Melody Maker*, writing on the same album, describes it as a 'particularly difficult album to come to any firm

conclusion on . . . It's late night coffee 'n' chat music', before listing
the supporting musicians, including John Cale, Paul Harris, Mike
Kowalski, Ray Warleigh and various members of Fairport Convention, as evidence of the album's quality rather than the music itself.[6]

By *Pink Moon* in 1972 the reviews were equally circumspect. Jerry
Gilbert, again writing in *Sounds*, berates Drake for his mysteriously
reclusive public profile, while reiterating the point that his songs
require dressing up to augment somewhat slight pieces of music.[7]
Mark Plummer's review in *Melody Maker*, while seemingly positive
about the album, suggests that:

> Perhaps one should play his albums with the sound off and just
> look at the cover and make the music in your head reciting his
> words from inside the cover to your own rhythmic heart
> rhymes . . . It could be that Nick Drake does not exist at all.[8]

Such ambivalence seems far removed from the praise generally
heaped upon Drake's music today. The review of *Pink Moon* in
Melody Maker mentions the pockets of appreciation that he did
gather to his cause, but clearly, since the mid-1980s, Drake's wider
audience has found something perhaps more enticing than even
relative champions of his music such as Jerry Gilbert did during
his lifetime.

Looking to the three core albums, *Five Leaves Left*, *Bryter Layter*
and *Pink Moon*, a body of work emerges that shows both contrast
and consistency. Broadly speaking, the albums may be primarily
categorized as acoustic in nature, although the term applies more
to certain albums than others. In reverse chronological order, *Pink
Moon* is Drake's most minimal effort, featuring only his voice and
acoustic guitar with that fleeting piano overdub on the title track.
Bryter Layter, recorded with a conscious view to crossover pop
appeal, has the broadest sonic palette, featuring drums, horns,
electric guitar, flute, harpsichord, celesta, organ and strings. Quite

how happy Drake felt with the more commercial production of his second album is unclear but there appeared to be some level of tension between Nick and producer Joe Boyd. Boyd comments that

> *Bryter Layter* is one of my favourite albums, a record I can sit back and listen to without wishing to redo this or that . . . John Wood never got a better sound and we mixed it over and over until we were absolutely satisfied. But when the album was finished, Nick told me he wanted to make his next record alone – no arrangements, no sidemen, nothing.
> . . . Nick, I think, felt left out of his own album. His refusal to include my favourite – 'Things Behind The Sun' – and his insistence on including those three instrumentals were his way of stamping his foot. His ghost is having the last laugh: the stark *Pink Moon* is his biggest selling album, while *Bryter Layter* trails in third place after *Five Leaves Left*.[9]

Drake's debut album, by comparison, sits somewhere in between, featuring a range of acoustic timbres from double bass to congas, with only one track, 'Saturday Sun', featuring drums and one featuring electric guitar (Richard Thompson's contribution on the opening track 'Time Has Told Me').

While the albums show a range of instruments and timbres within the Nick Drake canon, three elements stand out as being central to his overall sound: Drake's voice and lyrics, his guitar playing and the string orchestrations on the first two albums. Together they paint a picture of a body of music that betrays a cosmopolitan and somewhat internationalist range of influences and musical approaches. If Drake's music conjures up the verdant landscape of rural England, or the teeming heart of the metropolis, it does so using a range of styles that stretch far beyond these shores.

Nick Drake was writing music at an interesting time in British popular culture. *Five Leaves Left* was released two years after arguably the high point of British musical eclecticism – The Beatles's *Sergeant Pepper's Lonely Hearts Club Band* album – with Drake starting to pen his own compositions around late 1966 or early 1967.[10] While home-grown talent had managed to sustain a viable British pop music industry through the 1960s, the influence of America was still strong. The bedrock for Drake's position, as a peripheral part of the recurrent folk revival of the late 1960s, owed much of its existence to America, firstly through the development of a domestic skiffle scene in the 1950s, itself a scene evolved from the British jazz movement, and later through the burgeoning UK post-rock 'n' roll and rhythm and blues markets. By the end of the 1960s, hybridization and cross-fertilization between England and America was the norm, particularly following the British beat invasion of the States instigated by The Beatles.[11]

Such pan-Atlantic musical eclecticism was made an even headier brew by the effects of marijuana, LSD and an emerging psychedelic subculture in England:

> Psychedelia became an important touchstone for an entire generation (even if many never actually experienced an LSD 'acid trip'). When mixed with heavy doses of grammar school aesthetics and middle-class sensibilities it mutated into an aesthetic of embryonic pastoralism, not unlike that created and experienced by early [folk] revivalists such as [Cecil] Sharp and [Percy] Grainger. While the burgeoning counter-culture found it could tap into a cult of innocence and fairy-tale gardens, rock musicians also discovered that this fad of incorruptibility was a platform for musical conceptualisations of a rural idyll.[12]

The skiffle craze had brought with it not only an emergent interest in American folk forms but a do-it-yourself aesthetic that seemed far removed from the classically oriented music tuition that was found in Britain's schools at the time. While such an attitude initially allowed sometimes musically illiterate amateur musicians to find a stage and an outlet for their music, it also contributed to a wider sense of compositional and sonic experimentation (augmented in some cases by the use of drugs as a means of consciousness expansion). The results of this collision of stylistic hybridization, compositional and sonic experimentation and a broader strain of psychedelic culture were varied. Pink Floyd provide a useful axis for these connecting strains as, particularly through their early work, they form a body of music that, while heavily indebted to American forms such as the blues and jazz, evolves rapidly to provide a distinct British (or English) aesthetic that connects psychedelia to progressive rock through increasingly expansive and experimental compositional techniques and an exploration of pastoral and cosmic themes.

Nick Drake's music, while not the most obviously experimental of its time, nor indeed the most explicitly hybridized, sits well within this context. The acoustic guitar, the most central instrument within Drake's canon, situates him within a folk scene that, while often associated with pastoral Englishness, was looking back across the Atlantic as much as it was at home. While in the late 1950s Ewan MacColl had cemented a policy at his London Ballads and Blues Folk Club of performers only singing songs from their own cultural background, venues such as Les Cousins in Soho played host to a range of international and domestic performers who had a much more eclectic repertoire to choose from. The music of this period, be it by Donovan, Ralph McTell, Davey Graham, Bert Jansch, John Martyn, Roy Harper and many others, betrays little in the way of British or English cultural protectionism. It is music inspired by American folk and jazz forms, but it also looks to Europe, North Africa and the Indian subcontinent for inspiration. Equally, the development of folk rock as a form, particularly centred around Joe Boyd's

Witchseason roster of artists and Island Records, signalled a move away from the idea of folk music as something to be preserved in aspic towards something more dynamic, contemporary and internationalist.[13] The conservative ideology was moving closer towards that of conciliation.

Such a shift from the protection of folk culture in the face of modernity to a position where folk music opened itself up to both modernity and internationalism marks a move away from the largely socialist political imperatives of many on the folk scene from the 1950s, towards what Brocken describes as 'a growing attention to micro-level social processes'.[14] In other words, the lyrical and compositional focus of much of the singer-songwriter music that comes from this period marks a distinct shift in direction from the communal political role ascribed to folk music by MacColl, Cecil Sharpe and Albert Lloyd, and instead turns inwards:

> Performers such as Dick Gaughan, Keith Christmas and Vinny Garbutt all expressed deeply held personal beliefs. The music press (especially *Melody Maker*) described their like as 'singer / songwriters' rather than 'folk' singers (by now a rather archaic term). Singer / songwriters such as Cat Stevens, John Martyn, Al Stewart, Clifford T. Ward and Nick Drake became (and remain to this day) admired for levels of introspection hitherto unseen since the early days of the blues.[15]

Nick Drake's music certainly fits into what might be described today as a post-folk scene. It is introspective, highly symbolist and eclectic in its sources of inspiration. It is also worth noting that Drake did not see his music as belonging to a distinct folk tradition, even though many of his musical heroes had worked their way through the folk and blues repertoires.

While some of the songs on Drake's albums had existed for some time prior to their recording ('Things Behind the Sun' from

Pink Moon, for example, was written before the recording of his debut album), there does seem to be a progression that suffuses his work. The *Family Tree* album collects recordings made by Drake and his family at Far Leys between 1967 and 1968, as well as recordings of his songs made in Aix-en-Provence in 1967 and Cambridge the following year.[16] Alongside the fragments of family musical endeavours, such as Molly Drake's 'Poor Mum' and 'Do You Ever Remember?', Nick's duet with his sister Gabrielle on the negro spiritual 'All My Trials' and a collective family rendition of a Mozart piece, Nick's formative musical influences are readily visible. The album collects Nick's renditions of Bert Jansch's 'Strolling Down the Highway', Bob Dylan's 'Tomorrow Is a Long Time' and Jackson C. Frank's 'Here Come the Blues', 'Blues Run the Game' and 'Milk and Honey'. There is also a range of traditional tunes such as 'Winter is Gone', 'Kimbie' and 'Cocaine Blues' three of which – 'My Baby So Sweet', 'If You Leave Me (Pretty Mama)' and 'Black Mountain Blues' – Drake would have heard on the *Dave Van Ronk Sings Ballads, Blues and a Spiritual* album.[17]

The presiding impression to be gleaned from Drake's choice of covers presented on *Family Tree* is of a guitarist typical of his generation immersing himself in American folk and blues music. His interpretations of a number of songs from two specific albums, *Dave Van Ronk Sings* and Jackson C. Frank's eponymous debut album from 1965, point to a budding guitarist who has been devouring momentary musical obsessions to learn his craft.[18] However, while the guitar playing on the tracks is already extremely accomplished after three years of playing, Drake is far from a convincing bluesman. As Robin Frederick (who knew Drake in Aix-en-Provence and wrote 'Been Smoking Too Long', which he later covered) observes in the liner notes to *Family Tree*:

> Despite his mastery of the blues guitar vocabulary, no one could mistake Nick Drake for an authentic purveyor of the

blues! Rather, his fast, riff-filled guitar arrangements were perfect for entertaining friends or busking on the streets – the kind of thing that made tourists stop in their tracks and toss several francs.[19]

Particularly evident is Drake's mishandling of the pronunciation of 'cocaine' on 'Cocaine Blues', betraying his class roots as he sings about 'cockayne' blues.[20]

Drake's original compositions on *Family Tree* show the way in which he was starting to move towards a sound distinct from his formative blues influences. While tracks such as 'Day Is Done' and 'Way to Blue' would find their way on to his official releases, there is an interesting and timely suggestion of the way in which his music would develop in his cover of Frank's 'Milk and Honey'. While the version committed to tape by Drake has a very sprightly tempo and seems to owe a debt to Bert Jansch's guitar playing, Jackson C. Frank's original bears many of the hallmarks of Drake's later sound. In particular, there is a sense of suspension as the higher strings provide a thematic wash, while the bass strings propel the melody. Songs such as 'Road' and 'Which Will' from *Pink Moon* take a similar approach, while 'Hazey Jane 1' from *Bryter Layter* shows Nick's remarkable ability to sustain bass notes, melodic lines and higher vamps and riffs all at the same time.

If Nick Drake is to be understood as an example of a quintessentially English musician, or as part of an English musical tradition, then his influences might come as something of a shock. Given the lack of information on Drake's own views on the music and literature that helped to shape his own work, we are left with the recollections of those around him at the time to give some indication of why his music manifested itself in the way that it did. Patrick Humphries suggests that Drake was a fan of American singer-songwriters such as Tim Buckley, Leonard Cohen, Tim Hardin and Randy Newman. He also remarks that Nick was listening to

Love's *Forever Changes*, Van Morrison's *Astral Weeks* and the close harmony pop of Fifth Dimension. Brian Cullman, writing in *Musician* magazine, hears 'Van Morrison's *Astral Weeks*, Tim Buckley's jazz-inflected vocals, Jim Webb's melodic patterns, the sambas of João Gilberto, John Martyn's rolling, percussive guitar style', all of which Drake was known to have appreciated.[21] Joe Boyd mentions Dylan as an obvious source of inspiration, as well as the fingerpicking blues playing of Brownie McGhee and Josh White.[22] Other commentators mention Mose Allison as an influence (Mat Snow particularly hears his jazz piano influence in 'Man In A Shed').[23] Classical influences also played a part. According to Snow, 'Drake loved Debussy, Ravel, Delius and Vaughan Williams – [Brian] Wells remembers him playing a record of the *Fantasia on a Theme of Thomas Tallis* "to death"', while the final piece of music that Drake ever heard was a recording of Bach's *Brandenburg Concertos*, found on his record player on the morning after his death, and bought during his time in Aix-en-Provence.[24]

Nick had a particular fondness for Graham Bond, a significant figure in the British rhythm and blues scene, and he saw The Graham Bond Organisation at least once in London with his friend Jeremy Mason while studying at Marlborough College. Both Bond and Frank also suffered from mental illness during their lives, as Nick did (Bond had bipolar disorder while Jackson C. Frank was diagnosed with paranoid schizophrenia). Graham Bond died under the wheels of a train at Finsbury Park Underground station in London a mere seven months before Drake's own death. Artists such as Bond acted as important conduits for the importation and dissemination of jazz and rhythm and blues styles, even as they often shaped them into specifically anglicized versions of those forms. Again, the conciliation of American musical sources and domestic musical scenes provides a template for what Drake would achieve in his own career.

The breadth of Drake's listening tastes, if not his direct musical influences, are reflected in Paul Wheeler's recollection of the music played by Drake and his friends during their time at the University of Cambridge. Talking to Trevor Dann, Wheeler remembers an extraordinarily wide range of music being listened to,

> from the American jazz pianist Jaki Byard and the Dutch harpsichordist and early music expert Gustav Leonhardt to Smokey Robinson and Brian Wilson. Nick particularly enjoyed Randy Newman's 'I Think It's Going To Rain Today', Tim Buckley's mystical 'Morning Glory' and The Steve Miller Band's dope-infused instrumental 'Song For Our Ancestors' from their *Sailor* album. But he was also consuming modern jazz, especially Miles Davis and John Coltrane.[25]

This interest in cool and modal jazz is particularly evident in Drake's music. One of Nick's early musical interests was the saxophone, which he played in the Combined Cadet Force (a Ministry of Defence-sponsored youth organization present in many of Britain's independent schools) at Marlborough College, and the British singer-songwriter Keith James, who has performed concerts of both Nick Drake's and John Martyn's work, hears the influence of Davis and Coltrane in Drake's singing style.[26] A common characteristic of Drake's vocal approach is very long vowel sounds that float over the guitar chords as they shift underneath, while his propensity to enter a line late in the bar shares similarities to both Davis's and Coltrane's own playing.

The modal influence, focusing on melodic development over harmonic arrangement, is also evident in the guitar playing of Davey Graham, another influence on Drake, who absorbed North African and Spanish influences into his music – thus introducing them into the folk / acoustic repertoire – as well as forms of Indian music that had been encroaching upon the consciousness of hip music buyers in Britain since the mid-1960s. In *Pink Moon*'s 'Horn', for example, Trevor Dann hears the influence of the Moroccan music that Drake would have heard while travelling in his gap year.[27] Ian MacDonald hears Indian veena music in the song's reverberating strings and simple raga style.[28] Peter Hogan hears a Spanish influence, given that Drake had briefly visited Spain in 1971, just prior to the recording of the album.[29] Whatever one hears in just this one simple instrumental piece (and it is not alone in suggesting a truly international set of musical characteristics), it shows how Drake's Englishness is hardly constituted out of primarily English or even European sources. In acknowledging that fact, there are connections to be drawn between his music and the modal music of Asia, the modal jazz of the u.s. and the primarily modal forms of English ecclesiastical and liturgical chant and plainsong.

Such musical influences are sporadically apparent in Drake's music but it is hard to ascertain to what extent they informed his playing and songwriting. What is clear is that while the influences on Drake's composition may be highly internationalist and associated with modern forms such as jazz, the sound of his music evokes something much more specific, and at the heart of his music is his highly idiosyncratic guitar playing. His right hand alternates between strumming and fingerpicking, and it is his fingerpicking style that allows him to provide such a wide soundscape from one instrument. The recordings on *Pink Moon*, ostensibly just voice and guitar, show Drake's ability to not only fill space but to populate it with contrasting and complementary musical ideas. Drake's guitar playing is never merely an accompaniment to his voice – it often acts as a voice in itself, in much the same way as Drake uses his voice instrumentally, carrying melodic phrases that offset the vocal melodies. Listening to sketches of Drake's guitar playing alone, one can hear a range of melodic, harmonic and rhythmic ideas that flesh out a landscape of sorts.[30] When combined with Nick's vocals and fuller arrangements on the albums, this landscape becomes distinctly recognizable.

Drake's lyrics evoke a tradition of English Romantic pastoralism. While his music can be connected to both English and international traditions of music-making, it is the shape of the sound itself that most fully realizes a connection to the English landscape. While Drake's influences betray eclectic and cosmopolitan listening tastes, even if they are not particularly unique for young men and women of his background and era, their relevance to his music is oblique at best. What is evident is the sound of his music: a sonic landscape created through differing instrumental elements that together evoke the very fabric of place and situation. This is an evocation that summons up pictures of a variety of environments, all significant to the way in which England has thought about itself, and it is primarily through these sonic pictures that Drake's music most fully engages with Englishness.

It is significant that, despite Joe Boyd's preference and commercial hopes for *Bryter Layter*, it is the least commercially successful of Drake's albums. It differs from Drake's other two albums through its firm placement within a more urban and modern setting (both in terms of its music and its surrounding mythos and iconography). *Five Leaves Left* and *Pink Moon*, while very different in some respects, share an aesthetic that portrays a vivid sense of place through the sounds heard within the music. Instrumentation, rhythm and arrangement are vital here, and their work is not down to Nick Drake alone. The pivotal figures here are, of course, Drake, Boyd as producer, John Wood as producer and engineer and Robert Kirby as musical arranger. Together they crafted albums that evoke a very specific sense of movement, size, shape and colour which conjures up the very landscape that Drake's characters inhabit.

To be more specific, Drake's music evokes Englishness, or at least a somewhat specific aspect of the English landscape, through the treatment and separation of musical moments within the songs. This is usually achieved through the relationships between instruments, and is most fully realized on *Five Leaves Left*. Drake's debut album is in many ways his archetypal album, if such a thing can be said of such a small body of work. It is primarily acoustic, although Drake's singing and guitar playing are complemented by Robert Kirby's string arrangements and a range of other acoustic timbres. 'River Man', the 'sky-high classic' in Drake's oeuvre, is a case in point.[31] His ability to match his lyrical preoccupations with musical imagery is beautifully outlined here, as his lilting 5/4 guitar figures and Danny Thompson's sinuous double bass evoke the river flowing and bumping against the bank. The odd metre, seemingly inspired by Dave Brubeck's 'Take Five' (1959), evokes not only a river flowing but also the rhythm of the river as it laps against the bank. It shifts in an uneasy rhythm that is deceptively placating. Drake's voice hovers above the sound of his guitar and the soothing rumble of Thompson's bass, perhaps placing the singer above the water, on the bank. This sense of distance contributes to the singer's potential detachment from the river and all that it represents: transcendence, death, individuation, nirvana. Drake's long vowel sounds add to this sense of suspension as the rhythms of the guitar and bass undulate under his vocal melody. One might almost imagine Drake's voice as a boat gently riding on top of the water if the lyrics did not suggest that he was intrinsically removed from the water and decidedly land-bound.

When the strings swell gently into the song at 0:53 seconds, a further sense of suspension is achieved, although it is one sometimes at odds with Drake's vocal melody. The song itself alternates between minor and major keys throughout and the strings provide wide swathes of light and shade that, when factored into the aural landscape, seem to evoke light filtering through clouds.[32] The strings, orchestrated by Harry Robinson on this particular track rather than Kirby, provide the final spatial element of the track, adding a wonderfully dynamic sense of

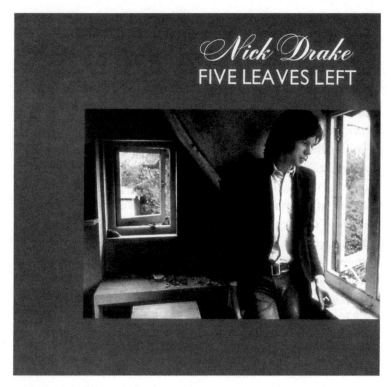

The front cover of *Five Leaves Left*.

mood and space to the rhythms of the rest of the instrumentation
and Drake's voice caught between earth and sky. While Robert
Kirby, a friend of Nick's from Cambridge, was drafted in to
orchestrate most of *Five Leaves Left* after an abortive attempt with
the arranger Richard Hewson failed to yield the results that Nick
imagined, he felt unable to adequately translate Drake's ideas for
'River Man' into a string arrangement. Robinson's background
in film and television scores seems to have provided him with
entirely the right atmospheric approach to the track, as the strings
harmonize with the guitar chords in the verse before sounding
a tremulous and ominous tone at the end of the vocal part.

Between the verses, two descending lines slide out of rhythm with the guitars. The first is high and bright, while the second, played much lower in range, gives both a sense of darkness and foreboding as well as a sense of light settling on the landscape. The strings here act as the clouded sky, shifting between bright beams of warm sunlight and overcast shadows. When the strings return after a short pause at 2:12, they are high and tremulous, mirroring Betty's desire for the sky to blow away. Here the sky is troubled, still bright, but the clouds are breaking up in the breeze. A pairing of the strings and the guitar at 2:32 provides a brief moment of harmony, but it is quickly followed by another tremulous swell that suggests unease, a colder wind perhaps, blowing across the water. The strings return to their earlier harmonious incarnation for the final verse, but resort in the last instance to one more uncertain oscillating swell before casting brooding abstract shapes over the final lines of the song.

This crafting of a sonic landscape through Drake's music seems a recurrent feature of his work. 'Three Hours' evokes the restless spirit of train journeys between Marlborough and London undertaken by Drake and his school friends, noteably Jeremy Mason, who is obliquely namechecked in the song. Its restless guitar and Thompson's bubbling bass provide a sense of movement as vivid as Neu!'s *motorik* rhythms, or more particularly the train songs of the American hobo tradition that no doubt inspired the song. Kirby's string arrangement for 'Way to Blue', the only instrumentation on the track, evokes a room of wood panels and perpendicular lines in its soft angularity. 'Thoughts of Mary Jane' illustrates this sonic articulation of landscape through Drake's fingerpicked arpeggios and the descending flute patterns which provide a sensation of wood and air, a gentle breeze rustling the leaves. Here the strings act to ground the music, a woodland floor across which the light dapples through the branches of Drake's guitar figures.

Bryter Layter is no less evocative of place, but it is a different place and one that fits in less obviously with first impressions of Drake's music. Joe Boyd's intention to make Drake's second album more accessible in sound results in a much wider variety of sonic textures and timbres which in turn evoke a space that oscillates between the country and the town. While the three instrumental tracks ('Introduction', 'Bryter Layter' and 'Sunday') have received little in the way of attention from those who have already written on Drake's music, they do chart the transition being made on the album as a whole. 'Introduction' opens the album and starts as *Five Leaves Left* ends. Drake's unmistakable guitar arpeggios, supported by Robert Kirby's string section, could be straight from his first album, and again a sense of separation, of distinct yet complementary ideas, is played out. Even the drums intrude little on what seems perhaps one of Drake's most pastoral pieces.

The final instrumental, 'Sunday', marks a dialogue between Drake's more exclusively European sound evident on the first album and a more distinct jazz influence. Ray Warleigh's flute, which acts as the significant voice in the track, again evokes a sense of light or breeze meandering among the branches of Drake's guitar figures, which are relatively unobtrusive. By the time that the strings enter at 0:45, the rhythm has picked up, providing a more contemporary rock beat with a hint of swing. After a moment's breath at 1:19, the flute returns with a much more fluid line, sounding far more of its time than the earlier, almost medieval lines. By 2:36 Warleigh's jazz background is in full evidence as he moves nimbly around Drake's supporting rhythm guitar. A final return to the straight figures of the opening section mark a return to a distinctly more English sound.

'Bryter Layter', which on the original vinyl pressing would have opened the second side of the album, is the most distinctly contemporary track among the instrumentals. Again the flute, this time played by Lynn Dobson, is the primary voice before the strings arrive with a jaunty melody that would not sound out of place as a television theme tune. Indeed the main criticism of Drake's instrumentals has tended to be that they sound very much like music scored for television or even muzak. Trevor Dann says of the instrumental tracks:

> The opening flute melody [to 'Bryter Layter'] sounds like the signature tune to an ancient BBC radio series or the sound-track to an education programme about wild flowers . . . Supermarkets have played less bland music than this.[33]

Peter Hogan suggests that Dann's comparison to supermarket music might be somewhat unfair but that there does seem to be a similarity to a television theme tune. Certainly, had Drake lived longer, he might have had a successful career writing music for other media. Dann is equally disapproving of 'Sunday' and questions Drake's judgement in

> placing a likeable but eminently disposable piece of what film directors call 'library music' at the end of side 2 where rock fans expected to find the album's *meisterwerk*, its A Day in the Life or Are You Experienced. Instead we get more super-market muzak, good enough for a documentary soundtrack but an unsatisfactorily bland and insipid ending to an album of such rich emotion and deep torment.[34]

However one might feel about the instrumental pieces on *Bryter Layter*, they are certainly the tracks that date the album the most, in that they are the ones that most reflect prevailing musical trends of the time. Across the album as a whole, *Bryter Layter*'s more contemporary sound might account for its less popular placing in the Drake canon as it seems at times at a distinct remove from more modern ears. One might argue that *Five Leaves Left* hardly reflects the modern world, particularly that of the 1980s and '90s, when Drake's music started to gain a significant audience. Yet *Five Leaves Left* and *Pink Moon* do not sound as if they are attempting to replicate the sonic milieu in which they were made and are therefore temporally portable in a way that *Bryter Layter* finds much more difficult. Drake's second album sounds more of its time, primarily because it attempts to marry his less temporally identifiable sound with very specific 'modern' voices.

Two tracks from *Bryter Layter* illustrate the problems that the album poses, not only to modern ears seeking something more timeless, but to the relationship between Drake's Romantic aesthetic and modernity. If *Bryter Layter* is Drake's city album, this is something that is voiced in very specific ways, from the thoroughly West Coast sound of Richard Thompson's guitar and the pumping horns on 'Hazey Jane ɪɪ' to the jazz inflections of Ray Warleigh's alto saxophone on 'At the Chime of a City Clock'. 'City Clock' is one of two specific engagements with a more modern landscape on *Bryter Layter*, and it is the one that most fully realizes the image of Drake as the rural innocent lost at sea in the heart of the metropolis. The guitar, strings and voice so evident on *Five Leaves Left* are particularly softly accentuated on this track, with Warleigh's saxophone dominating the soundscape. Here the usual Drake characteristics are placed high in an urban landscape, connoted through the ascending and descending lines of the strings and vocal melody. Drake's position seems to be placed among architecture, rather than in a rural environment. The strings sweep up and down, providing the buildings and streets through which the guitar meanders unobtrusively. The saxophone, a sound distinct and at times at odds with Drake's vocal melody, marks a separate urban voice that seems to win out over the fragility of the lyrics. Its urbanity is constructed both through its sonic similarity to car horns and through its connection to jazz, providing a vision of London that is not only alienating to the Warwickshire lad but that is also dislocating through its connection to non-English space – in other words, the American city.

The second track to mark out a more cosmopolitan setting for Drake's music is 'Poor Boy', influenced by the bossa nova music associated with Antônio Carlos Jobim and João Gilberto, among others. Again, Drake's jazz influences are showing through here as the track borders on cool jazz. The piano, added on an impulse of Boyd's by jazz musician Chris McGregor, taps directly into the light and breezy mood that elevates the song above mere maudlin complaint. Indeed, Drake's self-mocking is evident on this track as Doris Troy and Pat Arnold enter at the chorus to admonish him for his introspection. Here the bossa nova arrangement and the inclusion of black soul voices may seem at odds with the rest of Drake's musical output, but they sit well within the more urban sonic landscape of the album, and in many ways it is the most forgiving picture of the urban experience evident on the album.

Much of the credit for the levels of separation between instrumental voices on Nick Drake's records that provide the sense of space so vital to his work must go to John Wood's work at the Sound Techniques studio in Chelsea, in London, which the producer set up in 1964 with his business partner Geoff Frost. Wood had a background as an engineer working on classical recordings for Decca Records and had met Frost while they both worked at Levy's Sound Studio in New Bond Street in London. Having decided to establish their own recording studio, the pair found premises in an old dairy building and set about ripping out the central section of the second floor to accommodate a double-height live room with the control room above on one side and an

The home of Sound Techniques in Chelsea.

office and workshop on the other. Initially, the double-height ceiling was a response to what the pair saw as the overly dead acoustic properties of many English studios at the time. On visiting the Bradley's Barn studio in Nashville, Tennessee, Frost was impressed both with the level of natural ambience that the recording spaces were afforded, as well as the relative simplicity of the recording set-up, in stark contrast to what seemed to be ever more technical approaches to replicating American production techniques in English recording studios. To this end, Frost and Wood laid down a minimal acoustic treatment to the live room at Sound Techniques and left the lath and plaster ceiling uncovered, which they felt would be good for recording string sounds.

Initially, the central double-height well was designed to accommodate string sections, but the sloping floor of the old dairy seemed to suggest other acoustic possibilities. John Wood remembers that

> the interesting thing was that the low end of the studio, where we would [ultimately] put the string section, had a sort of natural resonance around 500–700 Hz or something, and you would get this really big string sound from a small section. That was one of the things that I suppose we were quite lucky with or famed for in latter years, the string sounds on the Nick Drake records people are always going on about![35]

This large, differentiated sound, coupled with as much live recording as possible, and an acceptable amount of sound leakage and room ambience between instrumental voices, provided the levels of space and separation that mark out the aural spaces that can be heard on Drake's records. Without the input of John Wood, his records would have sounded very different, potentially eliminating the sense of space that the music creates.

If Nick Drake's music evokes a sense of place and landscape, it is not necessarily one that is tied to England. At the same time, both Drake's voice and the iconography surrounding his albums go a long way to situating his aural spaces firmly within an English context. There are few recordings of Drake talking. Instead, there is the odd comment as he decides what song to sing on demo tapes, or a briefly recited poem ('Time Piece' on the *Family Tree* album) alongside one longer monologue recorded early in the morning, seemingly after he had somewhat drunkenly returned home from a party. The voice that we hear is not far removed from the voice that we hear on his records, as Ian MacDonald notes:

Apparently addressing someone else (possibly a girlfriend to whom he meant to send the tape), Drake wavers between self-deprecating irony and genuine self-disclosure, speaking in soft and rapid upper-middle-class tones of how easy it is to forget 'the lies, the truth, and the pain'. It's a young man's voice and a faintly stagey one, like a confessional character in a scene by Terence Rattigan. (This accent had modulated into something less class-defined by the time he reached Cambridge.)[36]

Perhaps part of the appeal of Nick Drake's music is that his artistic voice is distinctly English, and in a very specific way. He sits between the opposing forces of an encroaching Anglo-American dialect heard in much British popular music from before the advent of rock 'n' roll, and a markedly regional and working-class voice that sought to distance itself from American hegemony. Feather-stone suggests that 'in 1934, *The Times* complained that the default voice of British entertainment had become American', primarily due to the influence of jazz on Britain's musical culture.[37] Performers such as Gracie Fields and Noël Coward might have engaged with this encroachment via a range of strategies including the adoption of regional accents harking back to music-hall traditions and an exaggerated version of received pronunciation couched in deep camp. Drake's voice is neither of these things.

In listening to Drake's speaking voice, it becomes clear that he is largely singing in an unaffected voice and as such he sounds quintessentially upper middle class. This marks him out from both his contemporaries (John Martyn's mid-Atlantic drawl or Martin Carthy's regionally inflected singing style) and those who came before him. The Beatles had briefly toyed with the idea of singing in American accents early in their career but decided against it, opening up a space for northern English accents to find a place on the radio. Earlier performers such as Tommy Steele and Joe Brown had tapped into the latent connections between pop and music hall to present a specifically working-class idiolect that would resurface most noticeably through punk and Britpop. But Drake's voice was neither northern nor working class. As Featherstone points out, from the start of the twentieth century, accent has been a site of struggle and negotiation, either between the official voice of England (which is largely where Drake sits in this picture) and marginalized regional identities, or between those regional identities and a dominant American dialect.[38] Those who have chosen to articulate the vocal mannerisms of middle-class England in popular music, at least in an unselfconscious way, are few and far between, and Drake is perhaps first among them. Two performers who are often mentioned alongside Nick Drake, when thinking about a specifically English (in other words, non-regional, upper-class) voice, are Colin Blunstone of The Zombies and Clifford T. Ward, who equally stand out as contemporary exceptions to the rules of Anglo-Americanism or regionality that have continued to be prevalent in one way or another for almost a century. However, it is this voice, representative not so much of a specific region as it is representative of a class system, and a class system that was undergoing significant challenges from the 1950s onwards, that marks Drake's voice out as not only English but of an England passing away.

When encountering possible representations of Englishness in Nick Drake's music, it is the sound that first impresses such images upon the listener. The collective efforts of Drake, Kirby, Boyd and Wood, as well as the range of musical collaborators on the first two albums, set the stage for the lyrical preoccupations and iconographic framing that comes afterwards. Where this is more difficult to discern is on Drake's final album, *Pink Moon*. Its instrumental sparseness limits the extent to which it is capable of manifesting sonic spaces, but as we will see, this album can be thought of in terms of an interiorized landscape that maintains connections to English cultural life in quite different ways. As Drake's first two albums show, the music engages with urban as well as rural spaces, yet to frame one as the negative polarity of the other is problematic. The town and the country in Drake's music form a dialogue that is of significance to the ways in which his music articulates Englishness, and the ways in which contemporary listeners find versions of Englishness in his music.

3 THE COUNTRY AND THE CITY

If Nick Drake's albums conjure before us aural landscapes, images both of England's rural countryside and a potentially more disturbing cityscape, it would be fair to suppose that the traditional view of Drake as a romantic pastoral troubadour would be appropriate. But the situation is not so clear-cut. Both the country and the city are presented in ominous ways by Drake's songs, but the city is a far more ambiguous space, both within his music and in terms of his biography. The polarity of the country and the city is far from clear, and while the Drakes may have lived in apparent bucolic bliss in Tanworth-in-Arden, the village was and continues to be a semi-rural, semi-suburban satellite residential area for Birmingham, England's second biggest metropolis, with its city centre a mere 14 miles away. Cambridge was also not quite the educational sanctuary perhaps envisioned by Nick when he went to study there in 1967. London, the backdrop for Drake's mental deterioration, was also a place where he made friends and socialized and it held a particular attraction to him in his early years.

While it may be easy to situate Drake as belonging to a tradition of Romantic poets or musicians, his music and biography paint a far more ambivalent picture of the relationship between town and country. It is this very ambivalence that lends power to Drake's dreaming of England through his music and his story, and is one of the factors that make his music so compelling to this day. As should be clear by this point, it is not easy to uncover any concrete level of meaning behind the words of Nick Drake's songs, such is the lack of detail to corroborate any inferences that might be made. However, such gaps provide two contrasting and sometimes complementary approaches to his music. Initially, one might choose to superimpose one's own memories or feelings onto the backdrop that Drake's music provides, or alternatively, one might look to Drake's own life for clues. While the latter approach may not provide any more certain a reading (if such a thing were possible) than any other contrasting views, given the number of words devoted to him in the biographies, documentaries and magazine articles that have sought to resolve the mystery that Drake represents, many listeners read Drake's music through the details that they know about his life. This is partly a product of the highly introspective nature of his work, particularly on *Pink Moon*, but it is also a recognition of certain musico-topographical features that resonate with places that we know Drake frequented. For example, the line about descending to the Northern Line on the London Underground in 'Parasite' has been construed as a reference to Chalk Farm Tube station in North London, which is the nearest station to Haverstock Hill in Hampstead, where Drake lived in 1970. Such clues are few and far between, but they do suggest that place plays a significant role in Drake's music, even if its articulation is obscure or at a remove from us.

If Drake's music provides us with resonant echoes of the English landscape (at least, a particular set of English landscapes), then his lyrics provide suggestions about how he felt about those spaces. As suggested above, reading Drake's music and lyrics as championing the naive simplicity of pastoralism and recoiling from the alienation of urban life fails to tell the whole story. Rather, the relationship between the country and the town is a dynamic one, and as Drake's aural landscapes are dynamic places, experienced temporally by the changing of the seasons and the weather, so too are his lyrics and indeed his life. Movement and transition are key to understanding Drake's music, in that he represents moments of negotiation and conciliation between competing mythologies of English national character. Drake's Englishness is far from the mythological England trapped forever under glass; rather, his music presents us with an identity negotiating the tensions between Romanticism and modernity.

The idea of Nick Drake's songs as static, comforting, perhaps even womb-like, might not seem so strange, given the sense of reflection that suffuses so much of his work, not to mention the subtlety of his music. David Sandison, who worked as Island Records's press officer during Nick's time with the label, suggests that this very stasis is part of Drake's appeal:

> The romantic, dead poet is a wonderful attraction for a lot of people. It doesn't matter how they got into him, as long as they get into him, and they discover him. As far as I'm concerned, he's a kind of little island of tranquillity, which is very nice to visit now and again.[1]

Yet not only does Drake's music seem to evoke a highly troubled mind, regardless of any mental illness that might have plagued the singer during his lifetime, it also represents a sense of movement and dynamism that reveals the tensions in English cultural life at the time that he was writing. Drake, despite the idyllic setting of his childhood in Warwickshire and his education at Marlborough College and the University of Cambridge, was, like many young men of his class and era, negotiating a point of transition, a shift in the way that England was thinking about itself, and this is reflected in his music and lyrics. Drake is not so much the rural troubadour but rather a nexus of connections that mark him out as not only of his time, but as being a means of reconciling the problematic levels of English identity that have ramifications right up to the present day. He is emblematic of upper-middle-class life and the legacy of

The house in Hampstead on Haverstock Hill in which Nick had his flat has been replaced by a brick box of flats, but the Victorian house to the left gives a sense of what Nick's address looked like.

empire, but he is also emblematic of countercultural bohemianism and existential modernity. It is this ambiguity that provides a way of thinking about English national identity as well as allowing for that identity to be voiced in a number of ways.

To best understand Nick Drake's voicing of both Romantic traditions and the tensions of modernity, one may choose to return to the places that were significant to him during his life. These sites hold clues to how Drake is positioned as a fulcrum between inter-related myths of Englishness. Perhaps the first site to examine is Tanworth-in-Arden, Drake's home from 1952 after the family's return to Britain. It is worth noting that Nick would have spent a significant amount of time away from Tanworth, initially as a boarder at Eagle House School in Berkshire, over 100 miles away, and later at Marlborough College in Wiltshire, which even on today's motorway system would take almost two hours to get to from Tanworth. But Nick spent the first five years of his life in England in Tanworth before leaving for boarding school, and the family home of Far Leys would continue to be a source of inspiration and a place of retreat for him until his death in 1974.

Trevor Dann describes Far Leys as 'the Graceland of the Nick Drake cult' and it is perhaps not just the house that focuses fans' attentions to the village.[2] Nick's family grave lies a mere five minutes walk from his home in Bates Lane, while St Mary Magdalene Church hosts an organ that features a sesquialtera stop donated in Nick's memory by his family in 1977. The centre of the village includes the archetypal arrangement of a small village green, complete with war memorial and the church just to the east, with Nick's final resting place just beyond at the far end of the graveyard. The Bell Inn (a public house) on the green features a repro-duction of one of Julian Lloyd's photographs of Nick wrapped in his Tibetan blanket, offering the camera a handful of magic mushrooms (a small fragment of the blanket is held under the glass of the picture frame like a religious relic). Since 2002, fans from around the world have gathered in this sleepy village as part of the 'Nick Drake Gathering' that takes place each summer to commemorate his music and life, while the quiet stream of visitors to the grave continues throughout the year.

If Tanworth itself seems to represent an archetypal English country village, one need not go far to experience the countryside that surrounds it. Perhaps the view that most visitors will experience

A glimpse of Far Leys, Tanworth-in-Arden.

that best represents the Warwickshire countryside around Tanworth is from the bottom of the churchyard, just beyond the oak tree underneath which Drake's ashes were interred. The graves thin out until, as one descends the shallow hill on which the church rests, one reaches a fence, beyond which the familiar patchwork landscape of central rural England is played out. Patches of trees, gently undulating hillsides and a network of hedges dividing fields and marking out roads unfurls before visitors and give a real sense of Nick's place in this landscape. This is no sprawling suburb; it represents a space that occupies the heart of England's rural idyll. Similarly, Far Leys backs on to fields and the countryside beyond and Nick would have grown up with the rural landscape as a constant presence.

As such, it is easy to see why the recurring motifs of flora and weather should be so strong in his work. Travelling to Tanworth only adds to the idea of Drake as rural troubadour, yet Tanworth, as with many beautiful villages and market towns in relative proximity to urban centres, is no longer a rural hamlet. As Dann points out, Tanworth is an expensive place to live, and one need only look at the subtly imposing grandeur of Far Leys to see that the Drakes would not have settled there cheaply. As Gabrielle Drake recalls, 'I remember Mum telling me that the price of the house had been way above their budget, costing a shocking £10,000 [approximately £750,000 in 2013]. But she adored Far Leys, and Dad was determined to get it for her.'[3] Trevor Dann tells us,

> The house itself, with its Georgian windows and rather over-stated portico above a front door guarded by two potted conifers, was built for a prosperous Midlands doctor. Rodney Drake bought it from Jim Smith, a stockbroker with Albert E. Sharpe in Birmingham, who allowed a Miss Tonks to run a pre-school playgroup there before the Drakes arrived.[4]

After Rodney and Molly's death, the house became the home of a property developer, cementing the house's connections to the prosperous upper middle classes. The rest of Tanworth is not so different. The village, like many others, has continued to act as a rural bolt-hole for commuters and professionals, and this was no less the case when Nick and his family moved there in 1952.

If Tanworth represents the country in Drake's mythos, it is a particular kind of relationship to the country. The first thing to note is that it sits within a particular type of English landscape. This is not the dramatic bleakness of the northern or southwestern moors or the grand mountainscapes of the Lake District. It is almost as far removed from the coast as it is possible to be in England (Meriden, only fifteen miles to the northeast of Tanworth, has claimed to be the geographical centre of England for over 500 years, although this is disputed by other neighbouring locations), and the landscape marks the compartmentalization of the countryside following the Enclosure Acts passed between 1760

Marlborough College.

and 1820, which cordoned off much of what had previously been common arable land, leaving a series of divided fields and pastures largely controlled by the landed aristocracy. The vista at the bottom of the churchyard, while in many ways bucolic and quintessentially English, bears the marks of man's control of nature and of the tensions between the classes, which had fought one another over property and other rights connected with the countryside since the Middle Ages. While this is not an exclusive landscape, it is one that fits in very well with the Drake family's social position and with the upper-middle-class populace of Tanworth to this day.

Marlborough College, Nick Drake's school between 1962 and 1966, equally conflates a semi-rural landscape with a particular class position, at least in relation to his time there. Situated on the road between Bath and London, the market town of Marlborough sits somewhere between the tranquillity of Tanworth and the bustle of larger towns. On the outskirts of the town sits Marlborough College, a public school set up in 1843 primarily to educate the sons of clergy. While Marlborough College has its fair share of distinguished alumni (including the artist and writer William Morris, the poets Sir John Betjeman and Siegfried Sassoon, the musician Chris de Burgh, who almost joined a band with Drake, the actor James Mason, Kate Middleton – now HRH the Duchess of Cambridge – HRH Princess Eugenie of York and Samantha Cameron, wife of the current British prime minister David Cameron, as well as a plethora of distinguished names in politics, sport and the armed forces), it has never had the profile of more distinguished public schools such as Eton, Rugby or Harrow. Indeed, in its early years Marlborough had a reputation as somewhere to send errant young men to straighten them out into reputable adults, and its fees marked it out as a more affordable version of the public school system.

It was while at Marlborough College that Drake developed his musical skills. When he attended Marlborough in 1962, Nick was already a relatively accomplished pianist and he soon adopted the clarinet before moving on to the saxophone. It was in this environment that he started to concentrate on his musical interests, largely rejecting his early and accomplished interest in sport (which was the primary focus of school life at Marlborough). His first live performance, providing piano, saxophone and vocals for The Perfumed Gardeners in the grand Memorial Hall prior to a screening by the student film society, included Mose Allison's 'Parchman Farm', showing off Drake's interest in jazz.[5] Indeed, while it might be supposed that the public school system in the mid-1960s was the ideal place to retreat into the benefits of an establishment education, Marlborough at the time was equally open to a range of more modern cultural influences. An edition of the student magazine, *The Marlburian*, from 1965 shows evidence of a student jazz society alongside one devoted to the works of Carl Jung. One student provides a poem dedicated to Françoise Hardy, the French chanteuse with whom Drake some years later intended to collaborate. Other anonymous contributions feature poetry about suicide and insomnia, exhibiting a strong strain of existential cultural influence. The film society screened films by French *nouvelle vague* directors, and Drake's childhood friend Jeremy Mason remembers rambling discussions with Nick 'about Balzac or Camus or Jean-Paul Sartre, and about jazz, Coltrane, Miles Davis. We actually did all that stuff – that's what one did.'[6]

During his years at Marlborough, Drake seemed to spend a significant amount of his time exploring not only the Marlborough Downs that surround the town, a geography not dissimilar to the one that he had left behind in Warwickshire, although one more redolent of England's prehistory, but also the town itself, particularly its pubs and The Polly Tea Rooms, which are there to this day.[7] It was also at this time that Drake started to make the journeys to

Nick's house wins the 1965 'House Shout' singing competition at Marlborough College (Nick Drake far left and inset).

London with his friends that would inform his developing musical tastes and inspire 'Three Hours'. Drake was not living an entirely exceptional lifestyle for a public school boy of his generation, studying with all of the academic privileges that a private education could afford (even if he did not particularly excel), while immersing himself in the waves of American and Continental culture that continue to influence British cultural life up to the present day.

If Drake's music conjures up images of the English landscape, it seems likely that Tanworth and Marlborough both went a long way to shaping that landscape. Drake's songs and their arrangements speak of the rolling downs and gentle hills that would have been the backdrop to his formative years. While landscape, weather and the seasons play a large part in Drake's music and lyrics, there is no drama, grandeur or ostentation that might suggest any form of extreme topography, even by England's standards. His music is that of Middle England, both literally and figuratively. It is music that takes up the space of a middle-distance horizon, of views shaped by man but still indicative of a sense of rurality that initially seems in opposition to the town and the city. However, Drake's lyrics shape what we hear in his music to provide an interim space between nature and culture, between the past and the present, between the country and the city.

When looking at the places that played a significant role in Nick Drake's life, it is easy to map a process of progression followed by retreat. The boy from the Warwickshire village settles into adolescence in a rural market town before upgrading to the relative sophistications of a university city and then moving on to life in the urban sprawl. The retreat, Drake's intermittent return to Tanworth from 1971, does much to add to the myth of the brutality of the city against the peaceful seclusion of the countryside and the family home. Such an image plays upon the pastoral nature of

The Memorial Hall at Marlborough College, where Nick performed with The Perfumed Gardeners.

Drake's legacy, but in doing so it under-represents the fusion of Romanticism and modernity in Drake's work and the tensions and problems that Drake faced in almost every location that he visited. This is most fully represented by Drake's time in Cambridge, where he studied English literature at Fitzwilliam College between 1967 and 1969.

The procession from public school to a prestigious university such as Oxford or Cambridge was to some extent expected at the time (and still is to this day), yet Drake's middling A-level results meant that he was barely going to scrape a place into such an

august institution. The condition of the offer made to Nick
by Fitzwilliam College – that he study in France to develop his
French-language skills– meant that it was at Aix-en-Provence in
1967 that Drake started to hone his musical identity and to mingle
with other musicians such as Robin Frederick and Colin Betts, as
well as other well-heeled young men and women from the higher
echelons of the British public school system who were similarly
cramming at the university there or merely enjoying the pleasures
of the South of France.

When Drake returned to England, he settled in for his first
term at Fitzwilliam College. The institution had been a college of
Cambridge University for only a year before Nick arrived in the
autumn of 1967, with the construction of its campus on Storey's
Way commencing in 1960. It did not have the Gothic grandeur
that one might expect from a Cambridge college; rather, Fitzwilliam
was a thoroughly contemporary campus, somewhat modernist in
style, typical of its initial architect Sir Denys Lasdun (perhaps most
notable for his design for the Royal National Theatre in London
and the equally modernist developments at the University of East
Anglia in Norwich), who was inspired by the work of International School architects such as Le Corbusier and Mies van der
Rohe, as well as the American modernist Frank Lloyd Wright.
To add to the demystification of Cambridge, Fitzwilliam sits on
the side of Huntingdon Road, which was at the time the main
throughway between the eastern port town of Harwich and the
Midlands to the west, and as a busy arterial route through the city
is hardly the stuff of dreamy contemplation. Drake's ground-floor
room at Fitzwilliam was a spartan cubicle, with a bed, a desk, a
shelf and a less than inspiring view of the fence bordering the car
park. It did not take him long to abandon it for a flat in the town.

Yet Cambridge was not only the site of his continued musical
development after Aix, but his home while recording *Five Leaves
Left*. Drake showed perhaps even less interest in his studies at

Fitzwilliam than he had at Marlborough and he left after having completed only two years of his three-year degree to concentrate on his music career in London. Nick was continuing to make pilgrimages to the capital, now not only to see shows and buy records, but to perform himself, most notably at the Roundhouse in Chalk Farm. Drake's performance in February 1968 was the one heard by Ashley Hutchings, whose recommendation to Joe Boyd initiated Nick's professional career.

Perhaps Nick's most significant song to be written while at Fitzwilliam is 'River Man', allegedly inspired by the view of the River Cam as it passes under the footbridge at the bottom of Carlyle Road (Nick's home at the time) as it hugs the boundary of Jesus Green.[8] Cambridge is hardly highly metropolitan, even to this day, despite its significance as a university town and a centre for science and information technology. The city centre's commingling of medieval, neo-Gothic and modern architecture, connected by large park spaces such as Jesus Green and Christ's Pieces, as well as the networks of Victorian terraces that surround its heart, provide a strange melange of the past and the present. Cambridge represents both the wistful dream of a bucolic student experience and the utopian promise of modernity. It is Cambridge that most fully articulates what may be meant when Drake's music is described as 'pastoral'.

The pastoral tradition (perhaps 'sentiment' or 'theme' may be a more appropriate phrase) has its roots in classical antiquity, and continues to have a presence in contemporary popular music as well as most other art forms. It is a cultural strain that is rooted to the idea of the rural space, initially through its early incarnation as a poetic form in Greek and Roman literature that focused on the shepherd figure as a means of idealizing rural life. However, despite the enduring influence of the classical poetical form for many centuries after its heyday, the term 'pastoral' has come to denote something more widely connected to the countryside, particularly through its relationship to literary and artistic Romanticism. This does not necessarily mean that the pastoral, whatever medium it manifests itself in, excludes the city or the town; rather, it implies that one of the enduring characteristics of the pastoral idiom is its voicing of the differences between the town and the country.[9] It is a form born out of the very tensions between the countryside and its other. The term might also be used in a pejorative sense to suggest a highly Romanticized view of nature and the country that neglects the realities of man's incursions and effects. Drake's music, however, while certainly in many cases celebrating natural forces, always has the urban experience at its shoulder, if not directly in its view.

The distinction between the rural and the urban requires some questioning here. As Raymond Williams shows in *The Country and the City*, significant currents of feeling about particular spaces have accrued and become generalized:

On the country has gathered the idea of a natural way of life: of peace, innocence, and simple virtue. On the city has gathered the idea of an achieved centre: of learning, communication, light. Powerful hostile associations have also developed: on the city as a place of noise, worldliness and ambition; on the country as a place of backwardness, ignorance, limitation. A contrast between country and city, as fundamental ways of life, reaches back into classical times.[10]

Yet this contrast for Williams is no binary opposition; rather, the pastoral form marks a way of thinking about ongoing relationships between the city and the town as those relationships progress and mutate over time. It seems fair to conclude that Nick Drake saw much to attract him in London, be it the music scene, his sister

Nick's house on Carlyle Road, Cambridge, where he stayed after moving out of his room at Fitzwilliam College.

Victoria Avenue Bridge across the River Cam in Cambridge, close to Nick's lodgings in Carlyle Road.

Gabrielle, who was living there as her acting career developed, or his socialite friends such as Julian Lloyd or the Ormsby-Gores, whom he had met while in Aix-en-Provence. He certainly seemed happy enough to settle in the metropolis, even if his experience there was less than he had hoped it would be.

Drake's version of pastoralism works in a number of ways. As we have seen, the music that we as listeners hear on his albums offers us the possibility of an aural landscape; however, this is largely achieved in an arbitrary fashion. That is to say, Drake's

music is not mimetic in its representation of the English landscape, at least not in a direct fashion. The sense of movement
through time and space offered up in his work suggests certain
shapes and patterns that might be recognized in the landscape,
particularly those of the places that we associate with Drake, such
as Warwickshire. But he does not attempt to mimic the sounds of
nature through instrumental or production processes, as Vaughan
Williams does through his use of the solo violin as the voice of
the titular bird in *The Lark Ascending* (1914). Instead, in Drake's
work, instrumental voices evoke textures and shapes that may be
read as redolent of the English countryside.

However, to make the association between what one hears and
what one perceives it to mean, other factors need to be present to
suggest certain ways of reading the music. Timothy Foxon makes
the point that pastoral imagery is often associated with music
after its composition, 'via the marketing of the recordings, the
illustrations on the covers of composers' biographies, concert
programming, and so on'.[11] Drake's music might be confirmed
as pastoral through its use of natural imagery such as the sun and
the moon, stars, sea, rain, flowers, trees, leaves, sky, mist and fog.
Here Drake is often assumed to be tapping into Romantic literary
traditions associated with pastoralism and the primacy of nature's
innocence over the corruption of urban life. But it is also worth
noting that the framing of his music as pastoral has also been
achieved through the imagery associated with the albums on
their release.

The cover images for Drake's albums map out the progression
made by the music, even if he was sometimes unhappy with the
results. Keith Morris's front cover image for *Five Leaves Left* features
Drake staring out of the upper-floor window of a house near
Wimbledon Common in London, but it evokes, through the
trees outside the window, the peeling paint on the walls and the
wooden furniture, a sense of organic decrepitude that belies its

cosmopolitan setting. The cover shot for *Bryter Layter*, taken by Nigel Waymouth, is almost indicative of the pop orientation of the album by its very lack of specificity. Drake sits pensively on a chair that reportedly once belonged to Charles Dickens, his guitar on his lap and his loafers on the floor before his feet. There is the sense of a left-of-centre singer-songwriter, but little to place him in any particular context beyond that. *Pink Moon*, by contrast, features a Surrealist painting by Michael Trevithick, a friend of Gabrielle Drake's. Island Records decided not to use the shots Keith Morris had taken for the cover and instead went for something more abstract. While Drake does not feature on the record cover, it does perhaps hint at the interiorized landscape that the final album inhabits.

Virtually all the other images linked to Drake place him either within natural surroundings, or as a detached observer looking on at metropolitan settings. Keith Morris's pictures of Drake standing still while a blurred man runs past, and of Drake looking on at a speeding car on the A40 Westway raised dual carriageway in Paddington, West London, paint a vivid picture, one that is most fully realized musically on *Bryter Layter*, of the romantic country boy bemused by or alienated from the pace of city life and its anonymity. Other photographs, taken primarily by Morris, feature Drake in what appear to be rural settings, be it strumming wistfully at his guitar beneath a tree (taken in Regent's Park in London, although it is impossible to tell that the picture was not taken in the countryside), wrapped in his Tibetan blanket in Wales or stalking down the beach at Harlech in North Wales (both taken by Nick's friend Julian Lloyd).

The images used for the records tell a number of stories, but they contribute to Nick's aura of pastoral sensibility even when they are framed by the city. While the photographs of Nick in Regent's Park and the house on Wimbledon Common directly provide a sense of nature and antiquity, both a timeless sense of one's self in communion with the elements and a sense of time having passed. The more urban photographs taken by Morris consistently present Drake as an onlooker, detached from a world moving too fast around him. The image of the singer leaning against the wall of the Morgan Crucible Factory in Battersea, in South London, standing immobile as a blurred figure runs past, is perhaps the most significant image of him. Nick gazes to his right, thumbs hooked into his belt and legs crossed, unable even to look at the figure racing past such is his speed. Indeed, unused shots from the same session share the detachment between Drake and those walking past him. In almost all the photographs he is staring beyond the passing figures who similarly fail to acknowledge his presence.[12]

Ian MacDonald recognizes the framing of Drake as a detached observer when he suggests that almost all photographs taken of him seem to place the singer as a ruminative onlooker:

> Of course, most such portraits on singer-songwriter albums are similar, yet the equivalent stills of Drake are especially rapt and thoughtful. He posed himself in these ways, so conscious decision played a part; however, suggestions that this was all a matter of image-manufacture miss the fact that he genuinely was unusually introspective. Other young bards cultivated the contemplative image; Drake was the real thing.[13]

While one should not underestimate the extent to which Nick's image was consciously considered, the Morgan Crucible photograph and the accompanying image on the reverse of *Bryter Layter* by the A40 Westway suggest a difference of speed between Nick and his metropolitan environment. This is largely achieved by the blurring effect of a long exposure on Morris's camera, a technique that Trevor Dann suggests was potentially inspired by the photographs of Henri Cartier-Bresson, particularly *Behind the Gare*

Saint-Lazare (1932) which shows a blurred figure in mid-flight as
he leaps across a puddle to the rear of the Paris railway station.[14]
Morris's running man is similarly suspended by the camera in
mid-air, as if propelled by currents of energy that fail to catch
Drake as he looks on.

If the Morgan Crucible and A40 Westway photographs
suggest that the ruminative rural lad is marooned in the big city,
his innocence at sea in the hubbub of experience, then they situate
Drake as static. Yet movement is implicit in the images and provides
a context for Drake's engagement with both the city and the
country. In both images Drake is wandering the city, seemingly
without purpose. Whilst the factory workers hurry home, there
is no suggestion that Nick is similarly engaged. The A40 image
places Nick in an even more unlikely situation, staring away from
the camera as a solitary car, again blurred by long exposure, speeds
past. Here, Nick appears to be standing on the Harrow Road
flyover in London, noticeable for its lack of pedestrian access.
Quite what Drake is doing standing by the side of a dual carriageway suspended above far safer walkways is unclear, but he certainly
is not on his way to anywhere, just as he seems similarly adrift in
the running man photograph. While Drake is static in both images,
he seems to be wandering the city aimlessly, reflecting perhaps
on the drive of modernity as it unfolds around him.

The sense of restless wandering is supported by the lyrics to
'At the Chime of a City Clock', in which Drake likens the city to a
wilderness to be ridden, a flow of movement to be immersed in.
While the song also alludes to a reluctance to step outside the safety
of the home, a later verse again places Drake, or the song's protagonist, in a crowded square, searching for the face of a potential
lover among the anonymous urbanites. Once the glamour of the
city fades, the pair will leave it behind, fusing romantic love with
the implied pastoral idyll that awaits beyond its walls. The opening
track to *Bryter Layter*, 'Hazey Jane II', makes similar distinctions

Keith Morris's 'Running Man' shot, from the back cover of *Five Leaves Left*.

between the urban cityscape, a space so hyperactive that there is even little room or time to stare at it, let alone move through it, and the countryside, which is significantly painted as equally potentially threatening. The only recourse is to retreat indoors, or further into one's own head. But Drake's mythos is one of restlessness, not immobility. While David Sandison might be alluding to a sense of tranquillity suggested by the topographical landscapes presented by Drake's music, his lyrics suggest a sense of uneasy travel, as if Nick is propelled almost against his will into the city space.

Four years after Keith Morris shot the A40 photograph, J. G. Ballard would publish the second novel in his urban disaster trilogy,

Concrete Island.[15] The novel is a near-future re-imagining of Defoe's
novel *Robinson Crusoe* (1719), stranding the protagonist, Robert
Maitland, on a traffic island following a car crash, hemmed in by
constant streams of vehicles that pass by without ever seeing
him.[16] Despite his early attempts to escape from the traffic island,
Maitland ultimately seems to elect to remain there and forsake
his former life. The site of Maitland's marooning would have
been familiar to Drake and Morris, both of whom lived close
to the site of the photo shoot:

> Soon after three o'clock on the afternoon of April 22nd 1973,
> a 35-year-old architect named Robert Maitland was driving
> down the high-speed exit lane of the Westway interchange in
> central London. Six hundred yards from the junction with the
> newly built spur of the M4 motorway, when the Jaguar had
> already passed the 70 m.p.h. speed limit, a blow-out collapsed
> the front near-side tyre.[17]

Mike Bonsall situates the island that Maitland crashes into as the
circular interchange between the Westway and the A3220 West
Cross Route, a mere 2 miles to the west of the Morris photograph.[18]
One can still see the concrete spurs to the north of the interchange
that would have linked the Westway to the M4 motorway. Both Maitland and Drake, at least in so far as Morris's photograph seems to
suggest, have found their way into urban spaces that are simply too
fast for them to escape. Maitland, like many of Ballard's protago-
nists (most notably Kerans in *The Drowned World*), abandons the
trappings of civilization as modernity reconnects him to powerful
interiorized psychological forces that have long been dormant.
Maitland goes native in relation to the logic of the city, the car and
urban alienation.[19] Drake's response seems to have been to escape.

The connection to Defoe through *Concrete Island* hints at the role
of Drake's sense of movement and an implicit psychogeography,

both in the urban cityscape and in more rural environments. As Merlin Coverley points out:

> It is in his *Journal of the Plague Year* that Defoe provides the prototype psychogeographical report and, in the process, establishes London as the most resonant of all psycho-geographical locations.
>
> Defoe's fictional reconstruction of the plague year of 1665 was written in 1722, some 60 years after the event, and depicts London as an unknowable labyrinth, a blueprint of the city that was to form the basis for later Gothic representations. The successful navigation of such a city is dependent on the composition of a mental map, which can be transposed on its physical layout, but this mental composition is dislocated by the progress of the plague which renders a familiar topography strange and threatening. Here Defoe foreshadows the subjective reworking of the city that the Situationists were to promote and his figure of an urban wanderer, who moves aimlessly across the city before reporting back on his observations, has since become a crucial part of psychogeographical practice.[20]

The subjective reworking of the materiality of the city (a theme indicative of the work of one of Drake's literary heroes, William Blake) is crucial to understanding Drake's vision of the metropolis and the way in which it represents London particularly, and urbanity more generally, through his mythos of Englishness. Drake's experience is one of being swept up and aimlessly driven through the city, providing the impressionistic cityscapes conjured by his words and music. That is not to say that Drake was not writing about specific locations, but his music refracts those spaces through his own subjective experiences into something more intangible.

If Drake's lyrics suggest movement, it is framed either as a transcendent form of flight (as in 'Cello Song', 'The Thoughts of

Mary Jane' or 'Fly'), or as a sense of being carried along by currents beyond one's control, as in the examples above. While the flow of the city traps Maitland, the urban professional, Nick Drake is propelled around the disorientating spaces of the city as a *flâneur*. The *flâneur*, initially attributed to another literary inspiration for Drake, Baudelaire, is the aimless wanderer of the modern city, a relic of a bygone age impelled through the metropolis, both immersed within the crowd and yet isolated from any real sense of communality. For Walter Benjamin, the *flâneur*, at least as he is situated in the figure of the wandering wretch in Edgar Allan Poe's short story 'The Man of the Crowd' (1840), is very much a figure caught up by modernity and the 'unnatural' rhythms of city life.[21] The development of psychogeography, which takes its inspiration from Baudelaire, Benjamin and Guy Debord and the Situationists, often proposes the aimless drift, or *dérive*, as a means of uncovering layers of meaning that suffuse city spaces. Such an approach seems more than appropriate to understanding Drake's engagement with modernity in the city and the town. Yet, as suggested earlier, the city is not marked out as a space in the Drake mythos that is exclusively oppositional to the country. Drake's ramblings take place as much in the country as they do in the city, and while his nature imagery suggests the possibility of comfort and redemption in the rural, it is often at the same kind of remove as the urban landscape.

Drake's biography is threaded through with aimless wandering, both within England and beyond. Of interest are the extended car journeys undertaken by Nick, particularly in the last few years of his life, once he had returned to Tanworth-in-Arden. Molly Drake suggested that Nick was hardly any more at home at Far Leys than he was anywhere else, and would often disappear for days at a time in his car.[22]

Molly: I think driving was a sort of therapy to him; it gave him tremendous comfort. He used to drive for miles and miles and miles because – I don't think he drove particularly anywhere, but he just drove, and I think it was something for him to do. And of course, many times, he tried to go off to London, or other places, and he couldn't make it, and he used to come back . . .

Rodney: He'd sometimes drive out somewhere, and he'd run out of petrol, because he couldn't bring himself to go to a petrol pump and order petrol, for some reason or other. And then he used to ring us up and say, 'I'm afraid I've run out of petrol.' 'Where are you Nick?' 'Oh, I'm at the beginning of the M4,' or something like that, and off we'd go and pick him up and bring him back.[23]

Such aimless journeys manifest one last attribute of Englishness in relation to the pastoral. If pastoralism contextualizes the urban experience in relation to an imagined or lost past, then that bucolic idyll is something to be sought after and discovered. Featherstone notes how, during the growth of travel literature devoted to England in the first half of the twentieth century, many writers tended to neglect urban centres. Instead, the literature suggested an aimless wandering of the countryside as the perfect strategy to uncovering a 'lost' England, encroached upon by urbanism and modernity. Featherstone shows how many early twentieth-century British travel writers espoused the significance of almost purposeless travel, while one of the most significant of these, A. V. Morton,

claimed to have written *In Search of England* 'without deliberation by the roadside, on farmyard walls, in cathedrals, in little churchyards, on the washstands of country inns, and in many another inconvenient place'. 'It was a moody holiday, and I followed the roads', he declared.[24]

The writer and journalist Rob Young picks up on this theme when he points out that owing to Britain's relatively small geographic area, there has been no cult of the road within popular music to rival that of the American freeway or the German autobahn. Rather, travel, at least within the musical idiom exemplified by Nick Drake, is marked by rambling and wandering, aimless drifting through lost spaces and overgrown byways.[25]

Drake as *flâneur* represents not only the alienating effects of urban life and modernity, most fully expressed through *Bryter Layter*, but the impossibility of touching the transcendence represented by pastoralism. Drake's lyrics are suffused with a search for something always out of reach, and when the city propels him away from his goal, he goes searching for it, even if he has no road map. Here the myth of Arcadian England, of Cockayne, Albion or any other golden age, is always inevitably a goal that can never be reached. But perhaps Drake realized that the road to transcendence is transcendence itself, with no real goal at the end. In a quotation that Drake may have been familiar with, Lao-tzu observes in the *Tao Te Ching* that 'a good traveler has no fixed plans, and is not intent upon arriving'.[26] It is this sense of elusiveness, of something lost but almost recoverable, that continues to manifest itself through anxieties regarding urbanization, contributing to the myth of the pastoral that finds shape in Nick Drake's music.

4 MELANCHOLIA AND LOSS

Nick Drake's story is one that is inevitably tinged with sadness. This sense of sadness or melancholy tends to either be perceived in his music and lyrics, or connected to his legacy through his untimely death at the age of 26 and his well-known battle with depression. It would not be uncharitable to suggest that at least part of the attraction of Nick Drake's music is the sense that in some way he was communicating a very private sense of inner turmoil through his music. The perceived links between his songs and his biography suggest a brutal honesty that taps into articulations of authenticity in popular music. Similarly, Drake fits the archetype of the doomed Romantic poet, placing him in a lineage that includes Thomas Chatterton and John Keats, and one within popular music that comprises Tim and Jeff Buckley, Kurt Cobain and Ian Curtis, among others. These are young men, cut down in their prime, leaving a small body of work that did not have the chance to be sullied by the possibilities of later musical efforts. Having spoken to many people over the years about Nick Drake, the most common immediate response tends to surround his death, rather than his music – indeed, he seems to be more famous for dying young than for anything that he recorded.

Melancholy or melancholia, while by no means a condition or set of experiences that are exclusive to England and English cultural life, is visibly a theme that runs throughout the English arts, and it is a significant theme within the music of Nick Drake. However,

Drake's melancholia is often tempered by a sense of hope, of optimism, of the possibility of transcending the frustrations of daily life, either through a spiritual path or via romantic encounters and relationships (that may similarly stand in for a spiritual elevation).

This melancholic state works to represent facets of English national identity in two ways. The first is through a sense of loss, of something having passed. As we have seen, there is an idea of Englishness that is both closely connected to something that has been lost and, concurrently, an expression of that loss, and it is in this sense that Drake's songs provide a melancholic attitude that gives form to his 'Englishness'. Additionally, the connections made between Drake and Romantic traditions in English literature are in some ways cemented not only through the use of pastoral natural imagery, but through his manifestation of melancholia – a theme that is central to the English Romantic tradition.

What is attempted here, however, is not an attempt to directly engage with Nick Drake's battle with mental illness. While I will not attempt to posthumously diagnose Drake, even were I to do so, the facts surrounding his state of mind are unclear. We know that Nick, following a prolonged period of withdrawal seemingly initiated during his time living in London, was prescribed anti-depressants from 1971, and that he was briefly hospitalized following a breakdown the following year. His death on 25 November 1974 was recorded as 'Acute Amitriptyline Poisoning – self administered when suffering from a depressive illness', with suicide given as the verdict by the local coroner, Dr H. Stephen Tibbits.[1] Despite having taken around 30 Tryptizol tablets during the night, the verdict of suicide is far from clear. Drake left no suicide note, and the inquest into his death was conducted after his cremation, with only the family doctor's testimony to account for his death. Similarly, the exact nature of what was wrong with Drake before his death is obscure. Diagnoses of mental illness in the late 1960s and early '70s tended to be blanket generalizations when compared with the

Nick photographed by Keith Morris at Gilbert's Pit, Greenwich, London, August 1970.

relatively sophisticated approaches to what are now seen as a variety
of conditions, both physiological and psychological. As such, it is
not an automatic assumption that Drake was clinically depressed,
even if it is likely. Suggestions have been made that Drake was
suffering from borderline schizophrenia, and some of his behaviour
might suggest some mild form of autism. Potentially exacerbating
his condition might have been his well-documented use of marijuana. Dann makes the claim that Drake was also taking heroin
and LSD and further suggests that some of Nick's lyrics hint at
some form of childhood trauma.[2] Whatever the truth, it is likely

to remain largely unknown. What is clear, however, is that Drake's music conjures up a sense of wistful melancholy that has deep ties to the English imagination.

Peter Ackroyd's exploration of English culture, *Albion*, devotes an entire chapter to the subject of melancholy:

> In the nineteenth century London became known as the 'suicide capital' of the world but, even before that date, there was a more general belief that the English were a race subject to melancholia. The prevailing gloom was variously ascribed to the damp climate of the island or to the diet of beef, but we need only turn to the prevalence of elegies in the English tongue to suggest that melancholy may have found its local habitation.[3]

For Ackroyd, the melancholic strain is to be found in the earliest Anglo-Saxon poetry, focussing on transience, decay, desolation and *dustsceawung*, or the 'contemplation of dust'.[4] It manifests itself through the elegy, the lament and the dirge. Malory's *Le Morte Darthur* meditates upon the passing of all things, while melancholic themes run throughout the works of John Donne, Thomas Browne and Samuel Johnson to the more contemporary poetry of Philip Larkin and Ted Hughes. Ackroyd almost fully defines Drake, albeit unintentionally, when he suggests that by the late sixteenth century, the melancholic had become a stock literary device, clad in black, solemn-faced and disconnected from society. In musical terms, Ackroyd identifies themes of loss and grief in the music of Renaissance lutenist John Dowland:

> In songs such as 'Go Crystal Tears', 'In Darkness Let Me Dwell', 'Forlorn Hope' and 'Sorrow Stay', the full flood of English melancholia can be experienced, with all the sonorous languor of its pathos and all the chromatic range of its grief.[5]

In the twentieth century Benjamin Britten would return to Dowland's work, as well as the melancholic 'Lyke Wake Dirge', to inform his own vision of English music. Dowland is also often connected to Nick Drake. The pianist Christopher O'Riley, who has covered many of Drake's songs, suggests that within Nick's music 'there is an innate Englishness':

> The harmony can sometimes be simple, but it's very sensual. There's a real French sense of harmony overlaid onto what, in the English music history line, can probably be traced back to John Dowland and all the really great songwriters and musicians of the fifteenth century.[6]

Summing up the span and effect of melancholy on the English imagination is Robert Burton's *The Anatomy of Melancholy*.[7] Compiled and revised over the course of his life, only ever to reach some form of conclusion on Burton's death in 1640, *The Anatomy of Melancholy* was a compendium of writing and commentary focusing on the introspective and dour nature of much English literature and poetry up to that point. It would seem that part of Burton's rationale for writing this still influential work was to deal with his own depression (he is rumoured to have hanged himself), and it certainly privileged the need to examine the inner workings of the mind that would presage later developments in psychology.

One piece collected by Burton in *The Anatomy of Melancholy* is the tale of Lamia, which directly inspired John Keats to write his poem of that name in 1819. Indeed, it is in the work of the Romantic writers of the eighteenth and nineteenth centuries that we find England's most developed understanding of melancholia in a variety of guises. Burton's interiorized narratives would find a fruitful heir in the cult of sensibility that surrounds much English and German Romantic writing through this period.

Here spontaneous emotional responses were accorded as much importance as intellect or reason, and village folk, and the literature of antiquity, supplied models of experience that predated the civilized mask of developing bourgeois society as modernity took hold. Keats goes so far as to question the banishment of mystery via the illumination of science and 'cold philosophy' in 'Lamia'.[8]

Part of the interiorized experience for the Romantics concerned the appreciation and cultivation of melancholy. In melancholic reflection was to be found an intensity of experience, a subjective engagement with the world, even as it involved withdrawal. If Wordsworth, Blake, Shelley, Keats, Byron, Coleridge and others found the possibility of transcendence or even revolution through the celebration of nature (an aspect that lent significant weight to their evocation of the pastoral), the role of contemplation and inner journeys would provide a means to connect with the Sublime. As Jennifer Radden notes, the melancholy man was understood to be more sensitive and attuned to the potentiality of the Sublime, even while he may be tormented by an inner turmoil.[9] Radden's observation certainly seems to relate to Keats's 'Ode on Melancholy', written in the same year as 'Lamia'.[10] The ode takes pains to show how even within the beauty of nature, loss is always close at hand. It is the transient nature of the world that fosters the melancholic disposition, but it is through the appreciation of that transience that some form of reality might be comprehended. It says much that one modern usage of the term 'romantic' suggests a level of unreality or delusion, while Keats was keen to show that in introspection lay the road to the truth.

If Nick Drake's music is perceived to be melancholic, then it is in this reflective sense that his melancholy becomes attractive. While the Romantics might have believed that the immediacy of sensibility lay in the experiences of the ordinary folk, it would not seem impertinent to suggest that idle contemplation (even if it was to be understood as a vital part of the human experience) was not always available to all. The ability to stand apart from the pressures of everyday life, no matter what era one comes from, is often a luxury, and Nick Drake certainly represents a figure for whom contemplation and interiorized journeys were possible, not only because of his social class and education, but as a result of the relative freedom afforded him by his deal with Witchseason. Although never rich from his stipend provided by Witchseason and later Island Records, Drake was, like many professional musicians, afforded the space to create songs largely without the interruptions of a bustling family life or a day job. Whether this made any significant difference to the quality or themes of his output is hard to say, but as we have seen, much of the imagery associated with him plays on Drake's detachment from the world, whether it be as rural troubadour or as urban *flâneur*. Drake is free to play his guitar under the oak trees, to wander the streets of London, even if such moments of freedom produce feelings of alienation and melancholia. In this sense, Drake contemplates for us; is melancholic for us. He reflects on the world, seeing the possibility of beauty and the futility of trying to attain it. Nick Drake is our melancholic visionary.

Drake's melancholia, however, is of a particular kind. Ian MacDonald suggests that Nick's final album, *Pink Moon*,

> draws the gothically-inclined and repels the fearful. It's spoken of as bleak, skeletal, nihilistic, ghoulish, a suicidal plea for help. This grim view is unfair, the crowning misconception created by viewing Nick Drake as a troubadour of tragic sadness. He certainly went through his Dark Night of the Soul; indeed, he never emerged from it, and it killed him. Nevertheless he was a soul of light, a Romantic idealist – and this uncanny, magical record, far from bleak and ghoulish, is in truth a stark, sparingly beautiful meditation on redemption through spiritual trial. *Pink Moon* isn't about death, but about resurrection. A grave blessing on the solitary soul sundered

from the world by his or her sensitivity, it's religious music for our time.[11]

The album is certainly his most musically stark release, not only on account of the bare instrumentation – just Nick's voice, guitar and a brief hint of piano – but because of the sparse, almost fragmented nature of songs such as 'Horn' or 'Know'. But to paint *Pink Moon* as a wholly melancholy album is unfair. Indeed, the album's darker moments are often allied to lighter melodic and lyrical moments:

> Both 'Road' and 'Which Will' are melancholy without being explicitly miserable, a narrative trick Drake mastered early in his career. 'Which Will' seems cheery enough . . . until the verse's closing sentiments clobber the listener, self-skewering and hard: it feels a little bit like riding a bicycle, colored streamers billowing behind you, twisting your head to admire a few flower beds before smacking fast into a concrete wall.[12]

This tension between often rather bright musical phrases and somewhat darker lyrics is visible throughout Drake's work, from the opening bars of 'Time Has Told Me' through to 'Harvest Breed'. Further, much of Drake's music is relatively upbeat. Even on *Pink Moon* the title track has an uplifting musical quality that belies the song's sense of dread and prophecy, while the album closes with perhaps his most buoyant, optimistic song, 'From the Morning'.[13]

Yet *Pink Moon* is undeniably a dark album, and that it is his most popular effort in terms of sales perhaps suggests that there is something to its simplicity and melancholy that is of use to listeners. The mythos surrounding the recording of the album contributes to the way in which it is possible to hear the record. John Wood, the only figure other than Drake present at the recordings, recalls that the album was probably made in only two evenings:

Nick was determined to make a record that was very stark, that would have all the texture and cotton wool and sort of tinsel that had been on the other two pulled away. So it was only just him. And he would sit in the control room and sort of blankly look on the wall and say: 'Well, I really don't want to hear anything else. I really think people should only just be aware of me and how I am. And the record shouldn't have any sort of . . . tinsel.' That wasn't the word he used, I can't remember exactly how he described it. He was very determined to make this very stark, bare record and he definitely wanted it to be him more than anything. And I think, in some ways, *Pink Moon* is probably more like Nick than the other two records.[14]

Drake had been suggesting to friends almost immediately after the recording of *Bryter Layter* that his next record would be more significantly stripped back, keen, it would seem, to bypass much of the ephemera of recording and production to produce something that would fulfil an almost documentary role. What Wood and, by implication Drake, seem to be alluding to is a desire for *Pink Moon* to act as a conduit for the artist; in other words, for it to offer some form of authentic representation of the singer's inner states. Whether it fulfilled that desire one can never fully know, but what does seem clear is that, rather than following Boyd's previous strategy of gaining a larger audience by making Nick's records more radio-friendly, Drake was attempting to privilege some form of honesty over commercial imperatives. Perhaps his motivation for this change in tack was inspired by the blues artists that had been so formative in his teenage years. Equally, Drake might have been tapping into a well of 'authentic' expression informed by Romanticism.

While authenticity has been a constant site of contestation within popular music, Keir Keightley provides a particular trend

of authentic representation that seems to describe what Drake was
seeking to achieve with his final album. Honesty, directness and a
lack of mediation all appear as perceived markers of authenticity
standing in direct opposition to fashion, commercial imperatives
and formulaic musicianship. However, authenticity is never a value
that sits within the music itself; rather it is a set of values formed
in the relationships between music, socio-industrial practices and
audiences.[15] Further, authenticity can be constructed in a number
of ways. Keightley shows how both Romanticism and Modernism
inform contemporary notions of authenticity in rock culture and
popular music more broadly:

> Romantics valued traditional, rural communities . . . The
> Romantic artist was seen to be involved in a personal journey
> of self-discovery or fulfilment, through the direct expression
> of his or her innermost thoughts and emotions . . . While
> Romanticism locates authenticity principally in the direct
> communication between artist and audience, Modernism
> manifests its concern with authenticity more indirectly, at the
> aesthetic level, so that the authentic artist is one who is true to
> the Modernist credos of experimentation, innovation, devel-
> opment, change. Where Romantics see sincere, unmediated
> expression of inner experience as essential, Modernists believe
> their first commitment is less to reaching an audience than to
> being true to their own artistic integrity.[16]

Clearly, it is easy to situate Nick Drake in a tradition of
Romantic authenticity. His lyrics, throughout his work, seem to
speak through the singer rather than through invented characters,
and on *Pink Moon* particularly, the music seems so unmediated by
the production process that it is hard to see it as anything other
than a document of one man and his guitar performing.[17] Gone
are the landscapes produced through the intertwining of various

instrumental textures and rhythms; instead we are left with one man singing his own songs accompanied only by a lone guitar. However, the Modernist traits identified by Keightley also manifest themselves on *Pink Moon*. The album's minimal ethos, and particularly tracks like 'Know' and the instrumental 'Horn', point to a willingness to transcend traditional song structure, to mark out an interiorized landscape that portrays the mind of the artist with little regard for commercial imperatives or musical narrative. In this sense, Drake is connecting to the cult of sensibility most fully on his final album, even as he reconnects with Modernist impulses that most notably would have been found in the jazz records that he had been so fond of since his youth. Again, the tensions between the past and the present find some form of conciliation through Nick Drake's music.

The mindscape mapped out by *Pink Moon* has some level of consistency, but it is also marked by variations in perspective and intent. The title track, which opens the album, sees Drake acting as a prophet of doom, warning the listener of impending disaster. Exactly what the 'pink moon' signifies is unclear. Ian MacDonald suggests that it stands for illusion, while Peter Hogan suggests that it acts as an ill omen, or death.[18] Whatever it signifies, Drake has already seen it and it is coming for us all. This sense of inevitability recurs in 'Place to Be', a song that reflects on the pastoralism of his earlier work. Here the young idealist has been transformed by experience until he is older, weaker and darker than his younger self. As with 'River Man', the sea suggests a form of swamping, of envelopment, and time has not granted the song's protagonist any greater romantic skill; rather he is worn down by desire and eroded by life.

'Road' again juxtaposes competing visions. The addressee of the song maintains the levels of optimism and hope for transcendence that Drake's earlier work often clung to. Drake, however, is cast as the realist, a figure for whom redemption and transcendence are

no longer options, and have been replaced merely by the hope
of muddling along. This loss of optimism and vision recurs in
the album's next track, 'Which Will', in which Drake plays the
spurned lover ruminating on quite what he is lacking to secure
his love's interest.

'Things Behind the Sun', one of the album's key tracks, while
seemingly one of his darkest songs, acts as a bequest to the listener
to maintain some form of faith, even if that faith has let Drake
down. This song, more than many others in his canon, reads like a
statement of intent – that even if the transcendence hoped for was
never fulfilled, there is a value to honesty and directness. Drake
alludes to the difficulty of originality in the final verse, a concern
that Robert Burton shared about his own work, as well as the
disconnected sense of self that haunts his own behaviour (a form
of dissociation that would also manifest itself in 'Black Eyed Dog',
recorded two years later). The familiar motif of alternating major
and minor modes mirrors the ambivalence of Drake's own sense
of powerlessness and the promise that may be found in others,
and it is a bright, open chord that finishes the song with a sense
of hope.

'Know', 'Parasite' and 'Free Ride' paint perhaps the darkest
collective picture on the album. Using only a chugging, stripped
down riff, 'Know' lyrically is similarly minimal – only four brief
lines that hint as much at voyeurism as they do at devotion. The
reference to Drake not being there suggests the almost ghostly
presence many of his contemporaries felt he had become by 1972,
and the immateriality of the song (perhaps 'fragment' is a better
word) seems to mirror this sense of dissolution. 'Parasite' also
paints a picture of Drake as voyeur, regarding his own observations
of metropolitan life as parasitic, as the London crowd becomes
another sea of hopeless faces. One is reminded of T. S. Eliot's
'hooded hordes' in the final section of 'The Wasteland', or the
crowds of Edgar Allan Poe's London in 'The Man of the Crowd',

a mass enshrouded in their own aimlessness and lack of spirituality.[19] Even Drake's personal relationships are reduced in the final lines to a form of debased dependency. 'Free Ride', taken to relate to Sophia Ryde, with whom Nick had an on-off relationship, develops the idea of the final lines of 'Parasite' as love becomes something much baser. Here Drake identifies his unamed love as perhaps undeserving of his attentions, gilded as she is by the trappings of privilege, yet he still desires her. One might read the song as a recognition of the object's worth despite the 'tinsel'. Similarly, it is possible to read the song as recognition of the futility of one's own desires. Even though the object of Nick's affections is not quite what he imagined, he is still willing to throw himself at her feet for a 'free ride'. The latter reading says more about Nick's own sense of self than it does about the person he is singing to.

The final two songs on the album, 'Harvest Breed' and 'From the Morning', provide contrasting aspects of Drake's interior landscape. 'Harvest Breed' is characterized by falling – a complete inability to attain the heights hinted at in his earlier works – while 'From the Morning' could not be more different. Here all the optimism and wonder of Drake's earlier songs is reborn. The day and night are full of splendour; the ubiquitous 'she' is again the skybound idealization of femininity, and Drake and his listeners are bound together in the rapture of the Sublime. Were it not for the darker tones of the final tracks recorded two years later ('Rider on the Wheel', 'Black Eyed Dog', 'Hanging on a Star', 'Voice from the Mountain' and 'Tow the Line'), 'From the Morning' would have provided an elegant and wistful culmination to his recorded output.

There are problems with reading *Pink Moon* as a document of Nick Drake's inner world at the time of its recording. 'Place to Be', 'Things Behind the Sun' and 'Parasite' are contemporaneous with *Five Leaves Left* or earlier, so it would be fair to suggest that even if they reflected Drake's state of mind in 1972, they similarly might have reflected his state of mind in 1968 or 1969. The album is not a snapshot of the singer in time, but its immediacy and fractured nature do easily tie in with what little we know of Drake in the final years of his life. As Keightley points out, the authenticity of expression is not manifest in the recording itself; rather it is something that the listener can choose to impose upon it based on its lyrical concerns, its mode of instrumental delivery and the attendant biography of Drake himself.

If Nick Drake's first two albums paint aural pictures of recognizably English landscapes, *Pink Moon* achieves its articulation of Englishness in other ways. The Romantic legacy of sensibility and the value of melancholia provide a context within which to read Drake's songs. Were he an American artist, a generic style such as the blues might frame what he is doing with his last record, but, despite the influence that the blues had on him as an aspiring musician, there is little hint of it in terms of form to provide that context. The first two albums have provided ways to understand Nick Drake as a Neo-Romantic, or at least a musician for whom the imperatives of the English Romantics were influential – an assumption supported by what little we know of Drake's cultural tastes. Joe Boyd suggests that Nick's literary inspirations included Alfred, Lord Tennyson, and nineteenth-century English poets, although he is no more specific than that.[20] T. J. McGrath notices 'Chaucer, Blake . . . and Shakespeare' on his bedroom bookshelf.[21] Chris Bristow, Nick's supervisor at Fitzwilliam College, hears Tennyson and Blake in 'Fruit Tree' (Drake told his mother Molly that William Blake was 'the only good British poet').[22] There are also shades of Matthew Arnold and William Wordsworth in 'River Man'.[23] George Herbert, John Donne and Wilfred Owen also seem to supply inspiration, although the links are far from explicit.[24] Alongside these English literary connections lie Baudelaire and Rimbaud, whose work Drake 'discovered' in Aix-en-Provence, while Albert Camus' philosophical essay *The Myth of Sisyphus* (1942) was found by his bed on the morning of his death.[25]

Two questions remain, however. Of what *use* is Drake's melancholy and how does it connect to the representation of Englishness? It is perhaps not enough to say that Drake's music and lyrics are melancholic, much as the English nineteenth-century Romantics were, and leave it at that. Drake's blossoming popularity since his death suggests that his music serves some form of purpose, and that such a purpose might illustrate the ways in which his songs say something about Englishness across the millennial divide. The answer to these questions can be found in the way in which Drake's music straddles the experiences of Romanticism and modernity through the experience of loss. Following Freud's 'Mourning and Melancholia' of 1917, melancholia began to be understood as the inability to mourn the experience of loss.[26] Later psychoanalysts, particularly Julia Kristeva, understood the manifestation of melancholia as specifically caused by the inability to negate the sense of grief felt by the infant on the realization that the mother was a separate individual who could and would leave, and who would be lost. This original loss, never fully accepted or dealt with, might be assuaged by aesthetic or literary activities in later life that would both give voice to and keep at bay that primal sense of sorrow.[27] Such an understanding of melancholia shows how the artistic impulse may not only provide some form of therapy for the depressed person, but how readers (or listeners) might find some form of solace in melancholic art. It is this link between loss and melancholia that marks out the particular terrain of the experience of Englishness through Nick Drake's music. His is an experience of the loss of unity perceived to lie in the near past, whether that be read as the loss of the mother, or the loss of nature, selfhood or national identity.

While Kristeva's project, particularly in *Black Sun: Depression And Melancholia*, is to provide a means to treat melancholic or depressive states through psychoanalysis, Jonathan Flatley takes the experience of melancholy, manifested through Modernist literature, to be a means to map out the affective relationships between the self and modernity.[28] In this he is following Walter Benjamin's suggestion that melancholia was a historical effect of the transformations of modernity.[29] Flatley's identification of Modernist literature as a means of affective mapping of the experience of modernity is of use here, as it helps to define exactly what sense of loss is being experienced through Nick Drake's music and its relationship to Englishness. Flatley identifies the experiences of modernity – 'urbanization, industrialization, . . . imperialism, modern warfare, the invention of "race," the advent of the modern commodity . . , the emergence of modern discourses of gender and sexuality, and the pathologization of homosexuality'' – that writers such as Henry James, W.E.B. Du Bois and Andrei Platonov connect with through their writing, and many of those categories find a voice through Nick Drake's music and attendant biography.[30] The tensions between the town and the country, his family's part in the legacy of empire, the classed 'whiteness' of Drake's vocal delivery, his hopes and fears of the commercialization of his music and the troubled nature of his relationships with women, both in his life and through his music, all point to moments of loss or anxiety that are born out of the experience of modernity.

It is thus through the melancholic reflection of Nick Drake's music that listeners are offered the opportunity to reflect on the ways in which historical and social forces pull the subject apart from some form of imaginary origin. The music of Nick Drake is not that imagined origin, nor does it represent it; rather he is the embodiment of its loss, and as we will see, in that embodiment contemporary listeners can affectively map their own relationships to the pressures of modernity. This would be particularly significant, for example, for those listeners mourning the loss of an effective counterculture since the 1970s. Melancholia forms a space through which one can map out the roots of one's psychic life and share a sense of loss, whatever that loss may consist of, with others who might experience similar sentiments.

While one of the characteristics of depression is withdrawal and an inability to connect, Nick Drake, at least at times, was keen to make connections with his audience. While the sessions for *Pink Moon* and his final recordings two years later seemed to coincide with particularly dark times in Nick's life, Cally Callomon, who currently manages his estate, points out that during acute periods of depression Drake would have been incapable of writing or recording:

> He was not depressed during the writing or recording of *Pink Moon* and was immensely proud of the album, as letters to his father testify . . . Some journalists and book writers have found this fact disappointing, as it doesn't reflect their own impression of the album.[31]

It is tempting to see the melancholic strains that suffuse Drake's work as direct representations of his mental illness, yet they are far more than that. They are maps, not only musical maps of the English landscape, but of a figure born in a certain time and cultural space that was suspended between the perception of a more peaceful past (albeit one occluded by the very real implications of class, imperialism and privilege) and the congruent tides of modernity as they shaped not only the physical landscape of England, but the cultural terrain of Drake's aesthetic tastes. Such a claim would suggest that Drake's music should be inherently dated, yet its lack of lyrical specificity means that it acts as a strategy to negotiate similarly competing images of England to this day. Englishness might be understood not as a concrete set of traits, but rather as the experience of a process of negotiation centred upon dialectics of class, race, urban and rural space, multicultural-ism, the past and the present. In this sense, Nick Drake's music is

English precisely because it articulates, through melancholic reflection, an affective map of the social and cultural forces that continue to shape England well into the twenty-first century.

Amanda Petrusich offers a clue why Nick Drake's music may continue to hold some form of relevance to contemporary audiences. Commenting specifically on *Pink Moon*, she suggests that it offered consolation at a time of extreme trauma, specifically the terrorist attacks on the World Trade Center in 2001:

> I seized *Pink Moon* like a life raft, squeezing it too tight, curling up inside of it while everyone else I knew overindulged in work or booze or pills, trying to forget about human bodies falling out of buildings, bursting apart on airplanes, collapsing under the weight of half a million tons of steel and concrete. I wanted to consume *Pink Moon* until it was entirely mine, until I could have it forever, until it could keep me safe.[32]

Perhaps unsurprisingly, Drake's Englishness does not seem to be a concern for her. Yet, her use of *Pink Moon* shows how it acts as a locus upon which contemporary anxieties can be affixed, precisely because of the lack of any great historical specificity.

If a significant strain in English national identity is the perceived loss of a more concrete set of national and cultural values, even if that loss is largely illusory, as Raymond Williams shows, *Pink Moon*, and Drake's music more broadly, provide a means to reflect on that sense of loss. Drake might be the *flâneur* adrift in the urban landscape, driven out into the rain by dissociative voices, but he is also the melancholic free to reflect on his own inner sensibilities and map out the affective terrain in which he finds himself adrift. Nick Drake might have been sad, but he was free to experience and express a sense of dislocation, a sense that suffuses English national identity, particularly as it is understood in relation to pre- and post-industrial development. The Romantic cult of sensibility finds itself mapping out the experience of modernity as it morphs into Modernism in an aesthetic sense, and Drake is heir to that inheritance.

For the listeners who come to Nick Drake's music after his death, the relevance of his music may well lie in its ability to reflect on the tensions of a changing world and a changing England, even if that sense of change is manifested through interiorized psychic states, as they are on *Pink Moon*. In this sense, Nick's wish for his music to work for his audience has the potential to be realized. He represents the conciliation of the past and the future, of modernity and the pastoral, and as such, he hangs in the air, suspended by sometimes competing currents that continue to affect England and the rest of the world to this day. Melancholy itself becomes an attractive sensibility as it suggests time free to reflect on matters other than the economic downturn, terrorism, cultural homogeneity and class inequality (although it might be a condition which is dependent on a certain class position to allow contemplation in the first place). If modernity allows precious little time for contemporary listeners to achieve that form of reflection on their own terms, Nick Drake is there to do it for us.

5 DRAKE'S LEGACY

Given the growth in Drake's posthumous popularity, it is perhaps that which has happened *since* 1974 that is of more significance to the ways in which his music has come to stand for a certain type of Englishness. As will be apparent by now, most of the reflections on Drake's music have emerged in the years since his death, which seems to suggest that his music appears to echo a sense of Englishness that transcends his own era. Similarly, one might understand such comments as representing a desire for a certain form of Englishness, one potentially to be found in the music of the 1960s and '70s. Whatever the imperative, the uses of Nick Drake's music have continued to shape the way in which it is possible to think about what he left behind, and they have continued to cement certain associations between his music and issues of Englishness.

Nick Drake's recorded output during his lifetime was indeed sparse. Aside from the three official albums, we know that he also contributed guitar to *Interplay One*, an album of music, text and study notes intended for use as a teaching aid in secondary schools, produced by the educational arm of Longman Publishing.[1] Drake is also known to have played guitar on the Mick Audsley album *Dark and Devil Waters*, recorded, like his own albums, at Sound Techniques.[2] There were also a small number of recordings of Nick's music by other artists available during his lifetime. Fellow Island Records artist Millie recorded 'Mayfair' (at that point

Drake's version of the song had not been publicly released) for her 1970 album *Time Will Tell*.[3] Even a young Elton John recorded versions of 'Day is Done', 'Saturday Sun', 'Time has Told Me' and 'Way to Blue' for a Warlock sampler record in the same year.[4] A number of Drake originals also appeared on Island samplers through the early 1970s in a bid to boost his profile, although none of these extra-curricular activities resulted in any more significant exposure for Nick. However, they do point to the possibility of a career as a songwriter, had he lived longer. Similarly, the Millie and Elton John versions of Drake's tracks show how mutable his songs are in terms of delivery and interpretation. While Nick Drake's music might often be thought of as quintessentially English, his songs structurally suit the ska beat and bluesy Americanisms afforded them by these reinterpretations.

It would not be until after Nick Drake's death that his stock would start to rise, initially through accumulated word of mouth. Two songs relate specifically to him, the most famous of which, John Martyn's 'Solid Air', written before Nick's death, seems to anticipate the tragedy to come.[5] Richard and Linda Thompson were the first to reference the passing of Nick Drake in the song 'Poor Boy is Taken Away', released in the year after his death.[6] In print, a few extended pieces, working largely as obituaries, appeared, notably 'Nick Drake: Requiem for a Solitary Man' written by Nick Kent for *New Musical Express*.[7] Island Records's press officer, David Sandison, who had tried hard to get Nick noticed during his lifetime, also published a retrospective piece in *ZigZag* magazine.[8] By 1979 Island Records had released the *Fruit Tree* box set featuring Nick's three albums, plus the four tracks then available from his final recording session ('Black Eyed Dog', 'Rider on the Wheel', 'Hanging on a Star' and 'Voice from the Mountain' – 'Tow the Line' had yet to be discovered).[9] Again, this release did little to augment Drake's profile. However, by the mid-1980s, the cumulative effect of Nick Drake's cult was starting to become

more visible. Kate Bush, The Cure's Robert Smith and R.E.M.'s
Peter Buck were mentioning him in interviews, while The Dream
Academy's single 'Life in a Northern Town' had been dedicated to
Nick and much was made of this in the associated publicity for it.
It reached the top twenty in the UK singles chart and the top ten in
America.[10] The ensuing boost in profile prompted Island to release
the first posthumous Drake compilation, *Heaven in a Wild Flower*,
which would go on to sell over 20,000 copies in the UK.[11]

In the same year, Joe Boyd persuaded Island to let him reissue
the *Fruit Tree* box set, which had been deleted in 1983, through his
own Hannibal imprint. This incarnation included a number of
unreleased studio recordings, alternative takes and demo tracks
alongside the last four songs, culminating in a fourth disc that
would be released in its own right in 1987 as *Time of No Reply*.[12]
Further compilations would appear over the next two decades,
starting with Nick's contribution to the Island Records *An
Introduction to . . .* series of samplers in 1994.[13] The year 2004
saw the release of *Made to Love Magic*, again featuring out-takes
and alternative versions from the Drake repertoire, alongside
the final 'lost' track 'Tow the Line', which had been discovered at
the end of a reel of tape from the last recording sessions.[14] In the
same year, keen to capitalize on Nick's newfound visibility, Island
published another sampler under the title *Nick Drake: A Treasury*.[15]
Three years later the *Family Tree* album was released, providing
fans with a rare glimpse into the musical household that Drake
had grown up in, alongside recordings from Aix-en-Provence
and Cambridge made before the release of his first album.[16]

If the iconography of Nick's three albums had gone some way
to supporting the image of Nick either as pastoral troubadour or
urban *flâneur*, then the compilations and reissues did little to alter
that view. While this may be largely explained by the relative lack
of photographs of Nick, it is also played out in the graphic design
of the albums. Alongside the images of Drake reprinted in the inlay

for *Way to Blue: An Introduction to Nick Drake*, is the recurring motif of ivy, which is growing up a moss-covered wall in one picture. Here, the design by Cally Callomon situates Drake's images (and by implication, his music) as lost, to be discovered amongst the bracken, or the ruins of some derelict building. Similar images of decrepitude grace the inlay for *Nick Drake: A Treasury*, with the liner notes backed by what appears to be torn and peeling wallpaper. The inlay also features a wooden trunk, or tuck box, bearing the legend 'N. R. Drake. 69.' This motif is continued with images of a wooden box frame that opens in the central pages of the booklet to reveal the covers of *Five Leaves Left*, *Bryter Layter*, *Pink Moon* and *Made to Love Magic* alongside a shadowy image of Drake's acoustic guitar. Once again, Nick's music is presented as antique, waiting to be discovered. The box also seems to signal Drake's time at Marlborough and Cambridge, although the date would indicate the latter more strongly.

The idea of Drake's music as something lost, or at least archived for posterity, is similarly achieved on the *Family Tree* album. Here the nature imagery is absent, but the front and back inlay images suggest an antiquated photo album, an idea supported by the inclusion of family photographs of the Drakes inside. The red plush fabric of the photo album is worn at the sides, while ephemera such as one of Drake's broken guitar strings and a receipt or folded docket of some kind lie on top of it to provide a backdrop for the album title. The image behind the disc is of the track listing on a box of Scotch Boy reel-to-reel tape which features some of the songs featured on the album, with a Philips cassette bearing the handwritten legend 'Sgt Pepper:- Beatles + others' superimposed on top. The disc itself mimics a reel of magnetic tape, emphasizing not only the age of the material on the album, but the homespun nature of its recording.

The *Made to Love Magic* album continues the antiquated theme through its use of wallpaper designs in the style of William Morris.

Morris, himself a Marlburian like Drake, is now mostly remembered for his connection to the Pre-Raphaelite art movement and the instigation of the Arts and Crafts school of design in England at the end of the nineteenth century. Morris espoused a return to artisanship and craft in his design, and his wallpaper patterns continue to be popular in Britain, largely as a response to the influence of Modernist minimalism in interior design. Many of Morris's designs feature plants and flowers in vivid intertwining patterns, and the two samples included with the album bear all of the trademarks of the Morris Arts and Crafts style.[17] The idea of something being hidden is again played out through the simulation of a leather-bound book or wallet which, when opened, reveals a pad of Basildon Bond writing paper and handwritten lyrics to 'Tow the Line' and 'Made to Love Magic', while a wonderfully candid photograph of Nick smoking at a piano, taken by Victoria Weymouth, appears on the back cover.

The main image that stretches from the front cover of the inlay over five sides to the back is a composite image. It starts with a reversed black-and-white Keith Morris image of Nick standing by an *Evening Standard* billboard bearing the legend 'MANY YEARS AGO', taken at the Morgan Crucible Factory in Battersea as part of the shoot that would yield the 'running man' photograph from the back cover of *Five Leaves Left*.[18] Again, the blurred bonnet of a car glides past as Drake gazes down the street oblivious to its passing. The image then morphs into a tinted image of the Edmund Martin Ltd meat wholesalers in Lindsey Street, close to Smithfield Market in London, complete with an additional blurred figure, albeit a more modern scooter rider. The public toilet next to the Edmund Martin Ltd premises is merged into a separate brick wall which abruptly ends at a field under a portentous sky, reminiscent of the flat East Anglian landscape. A figure on the grass collects rubbish in a polythene sack, while the grass turns to tilled arable land before it too stops at the edge of a misty and indistinct sea.

The suggestion produced is of a movement through time and space, situating Nick within the flow of London, but a London transformed through the possibilities of the camera and Photoshop into a map of Drake's own movements. The sea, apparently disappearing into the mist at the far left of the image, suggests the transcendental dissolution hinted at in Drake's songs. The inlay itself, given its unique form, invites the viewer to read the image from right to left, given that the front cover, the first image seen, is of Nick in Battersea. As the inlay opens, the image dissolves to the left across the abandoned buildings, open fields and seascape, suggesting some form of oneness to be gained in stark contrast to the fixed, solitary figure at the start of the image. One final piece of ephemera, a note bearing the album title, is held by a paper clip above the *Evening Standard* billboard.

These images, all directed by Cally Callomon, add subtle nuances to the representation of Nick Drake after his death. A strong sense of a bygone era suffuses the compilations, from the abandoned tuck box and frayed photograph album to the reel-to-reel tape and ivy-covered walls. However, the *Made to Love Magic* inlay hints at a connection to a contemporary world through the use of colour tinting, the scooter rider and the modern dress of the litter collector. The images are still thoroughly redolent of Nick Drake's music, but they suggest a continuity of sorts between the relics of a past era and a similar topography still to be found, even if the manipulation of the image produces this sense of continuity in shorthand. In this way, Drake is situated not only as part of an English landscape, but one that is suffused with history, even if that history is decrepit or hidden. The sense of Nick Drake as an artist to be found or discovered is clearly articulated here, but there is also the suggestion that the English landscape, whether urban or rural, holds within it secrets to be uncovered, be it family photographs or abandoned trunks in the recesses of the home, or the legacy of obsolete urban spaces amid the changing topography of the modern city.

Nick Drake's music has also become more 'visible' through its use on television in recent years. Perhaps the most significant, at least in terms of the sales of Drake's music generated by it, was an advert entitled 'Milky Way' produced by the Arnold advertising agency in the u.s. for the Volkswagen Cabrio car in 1999. Following an abortive attempt to use a song by the Australian band The Church, a last-minute replacement for the soundtrack was found in Nick Drake's 'Pink Moon'. The advert features four friends driving in the Cabrio through the night as 'Pink Moon' plays in the background. The passengers revel in the feel of the night air blowing through their hair, while one raises her arms to touch passing fireflies. On arriving at their destination, seemingly a party or bar, they look on at the rowdy revellers and think better of stopping. The advert finishes with the car turning round and cruising back into the night. As Trevor Dann suggests, 'Nick Drake sold more albums in the usa in one month than he had in the previous 30 years and Pink Moon found itself in the Billboard Top 100.'[19] Soundscan data for 1999 / 2000 shows a marked increase in American sales of Drake's music. *Pink Moon*, which had sold 5,666 units in 1999, jumped, following the advert, to 74,696 sales, while the *Way to Blue* compilation almost increased its sales six-fold to 67,916 units over the same period. The advert also received the accolade of best use of music in an advert by *Billboard* in 2009.

A more recent use of Nick Drake's music in advertising also comes from the u.s. In 2010 the telecommunications company at&t used 'From the Morning' as the soundtrack to their 'Blanket' commercial. The advert features a series of American landmarks, including the Hollywood sign and the Hoover Dam, being draped in swathes of orange cloth to the wonderment of onlookers.[20] Both adverts share an ambivalent relationship to urban spaces to varying degrees. In 'Blanket', the city becomes a place to be transformed by the aimless use of giant rolls of cloth, signifying nothing other than the possibility of some form of magic waiting

to be uncovered as the city itself is covered up. 'Milky Way', although
decidedly less urban in its setting, operates a similar strategy
through the opposition of the hectic house party and the quiet
tranquillity of the four friends in their car in the night. While neither
advert seems to particularly foreground any sense of Englishness
from the use of Drake's music, they do both orient the music as
being indicative of a transformative event that reshapes urban
space, or that can be found in the solitude of a natural setting (even
if that setting might be found using a car). 'Milky Way' also hints at
the *dérive*, or aimless wandering, so indicative of Drake's own art
and life. These traits are not understood as pertaining to Englishness specifically, but they do illustrate the way in which themes
within Drake's work translate across national borders to achieve
similar ends. The transfiguration of America's modernity is represented by Drake's music in these two advertisements, whereas in
an English setting that very transformation would represent the
conciliation of past and present in ways that are of importance for
representations of English national identity.

In Britain, Drake's music has been consistently used to
accompany a number of television programmes. Again, the
framing of his songs marks out a specific context within which to
understand his music. Details of the full list of British programmes
to make use of Nick Drake's music are hard to come by, but,
particularly on the BBC television channels, one does not have
to wait particularly long to hear his presence. During the course
of writing this book, Drake's music has been used on a number
of occasions on British television. The rurally oriented BBC One
programme *Countryfile* used a portion of 'Hazey Jane I' to back
a segment on council tenant farmers in September 2009, while
its sister programme, *Country Tracks*, used the opening strains of
'Fruit Tree' in February of the same year. Both songs open with
Drake's distinctive guitar picking, and it is this aspect of the music
that is focused on. In both cases Nick's voice remains unheard

while the acoustic guitar and strings (in the case of 'Hazey Jane 1') suffuse images of the English rural landscape. Whether the music was chosen because it seemed to articulate aspects of English pastoral topography or not, the anchoring of the music by such images goes some way to confirming the link to be made between the songs and English rural spaces.

The link between nature and Nick Drake was again made on 12 February 2011 when BBC Two also used an instrumental segment from 'Fruit Tree' to back a piece on D. H. Lawrence's novel *Lady Chatterley's Lover* for the programme *Faulkes on Fiction*. Here 'Fruit Tree' was used to reflect on the primal nature of the illicit relationship between Connie and Mellors, a relationship forged in opposition to the restrictive civilization of her husband Clifford. While Drake's music played, images of budding flowers under-scored the implied sexual maturation of Connie and the pastoralism evoked by the music. Here the full flood of Romantic pastoralism made explicit links between Nick Drake's song and a more 'authentic' sensuality or sensibility to be found among folk culture, embodied by the gruff (although well-educated) gamekeeper.

Sometimes Nick Drake's music has been used to cement a more overtly nostalgic or defensive form of national identity in the media. In December of 2009 BBC Two used 'Hazey Jane 1' and 'Cello Song' as part of the soundtrack to *Delia's Classic Christmas*, presented by the television cook Delia Smith. Given Smith's reputation as a cook whose approach tends to favour simple recipes for home cooking and relatively basic cooking techniques over haute cuisine, the music acts as a connection to forms of 'authentic' or traditional national identity. Further, it is not only Drake's perceived Englishness that augments the show; it is also the status of Smith as one of Britain's best-loved celebrity cooks that augments the link between Englishness and Nick Drake. A similar use of Nick's music – in this case 'Introduction' from *Bryter Layter* – also makes links between the artist and a nostalgic

imagining of Englishness. *Michel Roux's Service*, also a BBC Two
production, used the instrumental track in 2011. The show takes a
group of disadvantaged youths and teaches them the skills required
to work front of house in the catering industry. Much value is
stressed in the programme on the value of dedicated work and
polite deference, acquired through the training period, and utilized
to, it is hoped, transform the lives of those involved. In this way,
the show seems to suggest that the perceived failures of contemporary society might in some way be redressed by a return to more
traditional values. It is notable that *Michel Roux's Service*, whether
intentionally or not, echoes the yearning for a return to a lost vision
of Englishness espoused by publications such as *This England*.

While the uses of Nick Drake's music on *Countryfile*, *Country
Tracks* and *Faulkes on Fiction* seem to evoke the connections to
nature often perceived in his music, *Delia's Classic Christmas* and
Michel Roux's Service hint at a more conservative ideology being
played out in relation to the songs. Heritage, legacy and tradition
are evoked between the programmes and the music, shaping each
other in particular ways. Here the use of Drake's music as a form
of conciliation between competing trends in English cultural life is
less explicit. The songs used articulate a version of English
national identity that neglect the more cosmopolitan elements
of Nick Drake's music, be they the influences of modal jazz or
bossa nova, or the Existentialist nature of many of his later lyrics.
Indeed, it is interesting how infrequently television programmes
use Drake's singing voice. There are of course practical reasons
for this, as viewers do not want to have to struggle to hear a narrator
battling against another voice singing in the background. However,
as we have seen, it is the sonic landscape evoked by Drake's music
that is of use here. Those familiar with Nick Drake's music might
add levels of resonance suggested by his accent and singing style,
or even by his biography, that add to the framing of his music as
'quintessentially English', yet equally, such extra information

might go some way to undermining such connections. Delia Smith, for example, has little or no connection to the 1960s English counterculture that Drake is associated with, while the focus on deference in *Michel Roux's Service* may be undermined by the knowledge of Drake's ambivalent relationship to his family and their legacy of class and empire.

If science fiction tells us more about the present day than it could ever hope to do about the future, one might also understand the manifestation of heritage, whether cultural, architectural or environmental, as a symptom of concerns about contemporary life. As the pastoral poetic form evoked a sense of loss that said more about aspects of urban life, and as the melancholic strain in English Romanticism suggested a concurrent tension within modernity, here Drake's music is used to represent a sense of tradition that might in some way solve perceived ills in contemporary English society. However, such a contextualization can only be achieved by framing certain attributes of Nick Drake's oeuvre over others that do not so easily fit such an interpretation. The possibility of understanding Drake not simply as an assurance of conservative imaginings of national identity, but as a point of conciliation between competing trends within English cultural life over the last century, relies on a different level of knowledge and context for his music than that offered by the instances mentioned above. But as with all cultural texts, meanings are shaped by context and Nick Drake's music is no exception.

Filmmakers have increasingly turned to Nick Drake's music to provide a soundtrack for their narratives, and here the value of English heritage is almost negligible. Of the 26 films that have used Nick Drake's music since the mid-1990s, fifteen have been American productions, two have been French, one Swedish and one Dutch. Six British or co-British productions have used Nick Drake's music in some form: *Driving Lessons* (Brock, 2006), *Me Without You* (Goldbacher, 2001), *Crush* (McKay, 2001), *Ratcatcher*

(Ramsey, 1999), *Hideous Kinky* (MacKinnon, 1998) and *Dad Savage* (Morris Evans, 1998). Of these six, *Me Without You*, *Crush* (alongside 'One of These Things First') and *Ratcatcher* have used 'Cello Song', while 'Pink Moon' appears on *Driving Lessons*, 'Road' appears on *Hideous Kinky* and 'Day Is Done' appears on *Dad Savage*.

What is noticeable about the various uses of Drake's songs in these films is a general lack of a unifying theme that contextualizes them as a whole. Many of the American productions – mostly romantic comedies such as *The Lake House* (Agresti, 2006), *The Perfect Catch* (Farrelly and Farrelly, 2005), *The Good Girl* (Arteta, 2002) or *Serendipity* (Chelsom, 2001) – use Drake's songs to suggest a level of romantic intimacy, but otherwise, any manifestation of an innate Englishness or even Britishness seems to be absent. In other words, the songs are not used in such a way as to articulate 'Englishness' as they are when used in the televisual examples given above. Even the British productions largely fail to use Drake's music explicitly to signify Englishness. It might seem reasonable for American films not to foreground the potential Englishness of Drake's music, but it equally seems strange that British films do not seem to use his songs in similar ways to their uses on British television. For the cinematic audience, both here and abroad, Drake's music seems to signify intimacy rather than any concerns about national identity.

To understand why such a shift in focus across mediums may be the case, one need only look to the documentaries about Nick. *A Stranger Among Us; Searching for Nick Drake; A Skin Too Few; The Days of Nick Drake* and *Nick Drake: Under Review* all play heavily upon the connection between the singer and the English landscape. *A Stranger Among Us* starts with a point of view shot from a car travelling down a winding country road, 'River Man' soundtracks images of punts floating lazily down the River Cam in Cambridge, another car shot scans down Haverstock Hill in Hampstead, London, while a third cruises past Far Leys. *A Skin*

Too Few takes such spatial contextualization to even greater lengths with lingering shots of the Warwickshire countryside, with some through the window of Nick's bedroom at Far Leys, and slowly shifting montages of cyclists winding down narrow Cambridge streets.

These shots are artfully constructed and tinted, the camera often moving slowly across panoramic views in time to Nick's music. In places, one is struck by how much the film owes to music video conventions, situating itself somewhere between factual documentary and artful pop promo. Trevor Dann recounts a review of the film in the *LA Times*:

> Given the alarming lack of material to draw on, Berkvens does a very difficult, admirable thing: his documentary often eschews facts and commentary to try evoking mysterious Nickdom. This stuff should be boring, but it's so beautifully measured and crafted that it carries a hypnotic, lyrical gravity instead.[21]

Nick Drake: Under Review is less ostentatious about the imaging of place, but it too cannot fail to concentrate on the locations so significant to the Nick Drake story.

Of course, such imagery is, in part, a necessity born out of the lack of any footage of Drake performing or talking about his own music. All the documentaries feature interviews with key figures such as Joe Boyd, Keith Morris, John Wood, Nick's school friends or those who knew him and his family in Tanworth. But the overarching presence is of the countryside and relevant sites in Marlborough, Cambridge and London. In the absence of Drake himself, his old haunts stand in for him, even though they have been transformed by the years since his death. Indeed, it is significant that such images underplay the extent to which these sites have changed. The Haverstock Hill shot in *A Stranger Among Us*,

Still from *A Skin Too Few: The Days of Nick Drake.*

for example, fails to actually show the bland block of flats that have been erected on the site of Nick Drake's bedsit. Whatever the motivations for such editorial choices, the effect is of a distinct engagement between place and his music. Given that the audiences for these documentaries might reasonably be assumed to have some interest in Nick's music, and perhaps some knowledge of his biography, the representation of place, and by extension Englishness, is more explicitly possible. While they may be attempting to uncover the truth of this enigmatic and reclusive young musician, they contribute to the iconography instigated by his albums, furthering the web of associations that conjure up a specific archetype of the English landscape and all that goes with it. In this way, the evocation of Englishness relies on the presence of the music, biographical knowledge and the presentation of both through the camera in particular ways. It is this method, used again and again throughout Drake's work, particularly after his death, that has done the most to confirm his status as a quintessentially English musician.

One is tempted to ask whether such imagery, further cementing the links between Nick Drake and the places he inhabited, skews

the picture. Certainly, the presentation of Nick Drake, first by
Island Records and Witchseason, and more latterly by Gabrielle
Drake, Cally Callomon and those associated with the media
around him, has consistently mined a particular seam that resonates
with elements relevant to how England might choose to view
itself, at least for a certain portion of its population. But it is too
easy to look back at Drake's three albums and see a cohesive
strategy or plan at work. There seems to be no evidence that
there was any long-term plan for how Nick might be presented,
or how his music should be understood. Indeed, the lack of
any coherent plan, at least on Island's part, might go some way
to explaining why he did not sell any more records during his
lifetime. With that said, however, the way in which listeners
come to Drake's music has been increasingly codified as certain
themes have been picked up on and extrapolated. As such, we
might see the dreamy impressionism of *A Skin Too Few*, for
example, as a visual equivalent of the way in which listeners, and
presumably the director Jeroen Berkvens, understand Nick's music.
In perpetuating and developing such themes – the countryside,
the dreamy university town, the isolation of London – the myth
gathers pace. But as with all myths, they are potentially of use to
contemporary audiences, even as they struggle with attempting
to represent a real man through such a small body of work and
information about his life.

While the documentaries on Nick Drake have gone some way
to confirming the implicit links between the musician and English
space, the use of his music by other artists has opened up the
possibilities for what it represents, both for non-English musicians
and for those for whom the 'Englishness' understood through his
original recordings is not so easily applicable. Drake's music has
been the subject of numerous tribute concerts around the world,
particularly in Britain and America. Sometimes these have been
individual artists such as Scott Appel or Keith James, who have

performed concerts of Nick's material to those who never got to hear him while he was alive. Larger-scale events such as a tribute concert organised by Peter Holsapple in New York in 1997, or the *English Originals* concert at the Barbican in London in 1999, have fused homage with the chance to reinterpret and re-experience Nick Drake's music.

In 2010 Joe Boyd curated a series of concerts under the banner *Way to Blue: The Music of Nick Drake*. The short tour, filmed on its final night at the Barbican for BBC Four, featured a loose collective of musicians including Robyn Hitchcock, Vashti Bunyan, Krystle Warren, Teddy Thompson, Scott Matthews, Kirsty Almeida, Green Gartside and Lisa Hannigan. Danny Thompson played double bass, while the musical director was Kate St John, lately of The Dream Academy and musical collaborator with Van Morrison, Julian Cope and Virginia Astley, among others. Whilst some versions of Nick's music adhered relatively faithfully to their original incarnations, others, such as Robyn Hitchcock's 'Parasite' or Lisa Hannigan's 'Black Eyed Dog', stretched the material in new directions. Hitchcock wrung effect-drenched sonics from his Stratocaster over the more conventional acoustic guitar backing him, turning the original into a far more overtly psychedelic event. Meanwhile, Hannigan's take on 'Black Eyed Dog', complete with foot stomping and harmonium, turned the original into an almost joyful Appalachian hoedown. Similarly, Krystle Warren's interpretation of 'Time Has Told Me' emphasized the blues feel of the song to suggest a far darker American aesthetic that seemed almost wholly removed from any form of English landscape.

What such reinterpretations of Nick Drake's music do is to divorce the source material not only from the accompanying iconography surrounding his music (although the backdrop to the *Way to Blue* concerts was the tree image used on certain incarnations of the *Fruit Tree* box set – arboreal references never seem to be far from Nick's music), but from the sonic texturing that does so much to connect to English space. Given new arrangements, and the differing vocal styles of the respective artists, many of Nick's songs seemed to bear very little relation to any form of English identity at all, emphasizing perhaps the cosmopolitan influences that shaped the music in the first place. While Drake might be understood as an 'English original', his songs do offer the potential to move beyond the places that Drake's legacy clings to.

Another example of how Drake's music is capable of moving beyond its status as particularly English is through the cover versions of his songs that have been recorded. Elton John's contribution to the Warlock sampler shows how, with the pianist's more explicitly Americanized idiolect, Drake's songs suggest entirely new vistas and panoramas that extend beyond the shores of his home country. Similarly, Millie's interpretation of 'Mayfair' hints at a different form of Englishness, one that speaks of the post-immigrant experience and the increasing influence of Jamaican immigration on British life after the Second World War. While the original collides Noël Coward with a ragtime sensibility, Millie's version, through its upbeat ska rhythm, heralds not only the potential re-imagining of London along racial lines, but also marks the possibility of a more multicultural England than Drake was ever capable of voicing himself, despite his disparate and internationalist influences.

Since those initial reinterpretations of Drake's music, and largely as a consequence of his growing popularity, numerous other musicians have approached his songs in a variety of ways. Some, like Damien Jurado's version of 'Pink Moon', remain largely faithful to their original counterparts.[22] Similarly, Danny Cavanagh's Nick Drake tribute album *A Place to Be* stays very close to the source material.[23] Other songs, however, have provided fruitful ground for more adventurous interpretations. Bands such as The Mars Volta ('Things Behind the Sun') have been able to approach Drake's music with a heavier sonic palette than might initially be supposed, turning his intricate guitar textures towards a more conventionally rockist direction.[24] The British rock band Drive ('Road') and American indie stalwarts Sebadoh ('Pink Moon') have pursued similar trajectories.[25] American artists such as Beck ('Which Will', 'Pink Moon' and 'Parasite'), by their accents alone, regardless of arrangement or instrumentation, have re-placed Drake's songs, or at least dislocated them from a specifically English context.[26] A similar example can be found in Lucinda Williams's interpretation of 'Which Will'.[27] Norma Jones's version of 'Day Is Done', despite its jazz-dive sensibility, featured prominently in the high-profile BBC Radio 2 documentary *Lost Boy: In Search of Nick Drake*.[28] Also, Brad Mehldau and Christopher O'Riley have separately transposed Drake's songs into jazz piano arrangements.[29]

Four cover versions of 'River Man' point to the possibility of situating Drake's music, not only outside the normative visions of Englishness, but also within alternative strains of English national identity. Norma Waterson's broad East Yorkshire accent situates Drake's song in a more explicit folk tradition, with long string motifs and drones holding together the piece almost without discernible rhythm.[30] One can almost hear Waterson singing the song unaccompanied as the music drifts lazily by underneath. Unlike the original, the music seems not to suggest the movement of water so much as bare moorland with its stark simplicity. Another northern interpretation of the song comes from Rachel Unthank and the Winterset.[31] Here Unthank sings the opening verse largely unaccompanied, apart from a scattering of soft piano chords. Unthank's Northumbrian accent provides a soft and unadorned setting for the song and, while her voice could not be more distinct from Drake's in some respects, it is this 'un-ornamented' delivery that evokes a simple vision of pastoralism, even if it is one that is less situated in the Home Counties (the counties that surround London) than it might be in the rural north-east of England.

Both the Waterson and Unthank versions of 'River Man' situate Nick Drake's song within a folk idiom. Two other versions dislocate the song in more dramatic ways. Paul Weller's version of the song, seemingly largely in debt to 'Tomorrow Never Knows' through reversed instruments and drones.[32] Even string sounds and piano parts drift in and out of the aural picture, sometimes heavily effected, often discordant. Weller's interpretation questions the Romantic basis associated with much of Drake's music, and reminds us that his musical tastes, and the era from which his music sprang, were often highly experimental or avant-garde, and it is through such a reconfiguration that Drake's music assumes a level of significance that stretches more fully into England's history of sonic adventure.

Natacha Atlas's version of 'River Man', musically similar to Unthank's piano-led interpretation, stretches Drake's Englishness in perhaps even more radical ways.[33] Atlas, a Belgian-born singer with English, Moroccan, Egyptian and Palestinian origins, came to prominence in the UK in the 1990s through her work with ethno-techno collective Transglobal Underground. Since then she has released a number of albums that have synthesized a variety of global musical influences. In her version of 'River Man', Atlas's vocal arabesques articulate a definite Middle Eastern sensibility, with some of the original lyrics, and variations of those lyrics, sung in Arabic. Here Drake's music is utterly transported from its English context into something that is more internationalist in nature and more reflective of the idea of England as something other than white and middle class.

The legacy of Nick Drake's music may well continue to play on the themes outlined in the previous chapters. In January 2012 Gorm Henrik Rasmussen published an updated and translated version of Pink Moon – A Story about Nick Drake, originally published in Danish in 1986.[34] Even from Rasmussen's perspective, the sheer Englishness of Nick Drake and his music resonates so strongly throughout the Danish poet's book, which acts partly as loose biography, partly as an extended tone poem, unravelling out of

Natacha Atlas.

one personal engagement with the singer. In the same month, the Idea Generation Gallery in London hosted The Strange Face Project, an exhibition of contemporary photographs of people listening to an unreleased recording of Drake playing 'Cello Song' that was found in a builder's skip in the late 1970s by the photographer Michael Burdett. The images of faces lost in contemplation as this performance, intangible to us as gallery viewers, creeps unseen and unheard from headphones to ear is frustratingly familiar. The dreamlike sense of transport provided by Drake's music is evoked as much by the contemporary settings of the photographs (and the contemporary faces of public figures such as Noel Fielding, Billy Bragg, Tom Stoppard and Fearne Cotton) as by what we imagine the subjects of the images are hearing. It seems unlikely that Drake will ever fully transcend his given role as a scion of Englishness, yet the mobility of his music suggests that it also provides spaces for others to reconfigure that connection, to update it or reinterpret it as desired. If Nick Drake's music can at once suggest a certain form of cosy rural Englishness at the same time as it suggests the impact of modernity, the cultural influence of America and Europe, the musical legacy of North Africa and Asia, existential bohemianism, the counterculture and its legacy, then there is space for it to connect with England as it embraces other cultural forms. Nick Drake's music was never exclusive nor protectionist; it was conciliatory, and such conciliation, whether that is between the memory of empire and multiculturalism, between straight and Beat culture, or merely between the past and the present, says much about why so many have flocked to his banner since his death. It is not that Drake's music is specifically English in any particular way; rather, we should ask why we choose it to exemplify Englishness. It is music that resonates in relation to the pitch of certain questions that the English might choose to pose to themselves. If Nick Drake's music seems utterly English, it is an Englishness that embraces so much from outside that it will no doubt continue to act as a way of thinking about exactly what it means to be English well into the twenty-first century.

Rather than thinking about Drake's music as part of some form of nostalgic heritage music, it is possible to consider his music as quietly revolutionary in its ability to enfold a mutable set of cultural forms and ideas, and to suggest new forms perhaps unthought of by Drake himself. His ongoing popularity might at times rest on a perspective that harks back to a previous decade, or even age, yet in that reflection lies the possibility of progression, even as the possibility of such progression seems increasingly remote once the records have been put away. As George Orwell puts it at the culmination of 'The Lion and the Unicorn':

> By revolution we become more ourselves, not less. There is no question of stopping short, striking a compromise . . . Nothing ever stands still. We must add to our heritage or lose it, we must grow greater or grow less, we must go forward or backward. I believe in England, and I believe that we shall go forward.[35]

CHRONOLOGY

Much of the documentary evidence that relates to Nick Drake is fragmentary and contradictory. Where explicit dates are available, they have been supplied, but many details of his life come via hazy recollections of contemporary witnesses, meaning that exact dates and details are often not attainable. The references to the live shows played by Nick are often based on adverts or bookings and are not necessarily confirmation that he actually played at these events.

1908
Rodney Shuttleworth Drake is born in Redhill, Surrey

1916
Mary (Molly) Lloyd is born

1930S
Rodney Drake joins the Bombay Burmah Trading Company

1937
14 April Rodney Drake marries Mary (Molly) Lloyd at St Mary's Cathedral, Rangoon

1942
January Molly Drake is evacuated to Bombay following the Japanese attack on Pearl Harbor weeks previously
February Rodney Drake joins Molly in Bombay

1944
30 March Molly Drake gives birth to her first child, Gabrielle, in Lahore

1945

The Drake family returns to Burma

1948

19 June Molly Drake gives birth to Nicholas Rodney Drake in Rangoon

1950

The Drake family leaves Burma for Bombay

1952

The Drakes return to Britain following the dissolution of the BBTC's operations in Burma. They settle in Tanworth-in-Arden, Warwickshire

1953

Nick and Gabrielle attend Hurst House School in Henley-in-Arden, Warwickshire

1957

June Nick enrols at Eagle House School in Sandhurst, Berkshire

1961

December Nick enrols at Marlborough College, Wiltshire, living in one of the school's 'Out Houses', Barton Hill

1962

Drake moves to the main campus site at Marlborough College to live in CI House, part of the mansion built for the Duke of Somerset in the early 18th century

1965

Nick Drake buys his first guitar – Nick's house, CI, wins the annual 'House Shout' singing competition at Marlborough College – Nick performs with The Perfumed Gardeners in the Memorial Hall at Marlborough – Drake passes his driving test
August Nick and friend David Wright hitchhike via Paris to the Côte d'Azur – Wright teaches Drake the rudiments of guitar playing – Nick returns to Marlborough to retake his A levels, following disappointing results earlier in the year

1966

July Nick gains A-level passes in English (B), British Constitution (E) and Latin Translation with Roman History (E)
August Nick holidays in Avignon in the south of France at the home of Jeremy Mason's parents

1967

January Drake travels to Aix-en-Provence to study French at the university, with friends Simon Crocker and Jeremy Mason
March Drake, Simon Crocker and Richard Charkin drive from Aix to Marrakech in Morocco, where they meet Cecil Beaton, Mick Jagger, Keith Richards and other members of the Rolling Stones's retinue, for whom Nick plays a number of covers in a restaurant
June Nick returns to England
September Nick arrives in Cambridge to study English literature at Fitzwilliam College – Drake meets Robert Kirby when they both audition for the Cambridge University Footlights Dramatic Club

1968

February Ashley Hutchings sees Drake perform at The Roundhouse in Camden and recommends him to the owner of the Witchseason management company, Joe Boyd
April / May Nick and Robert Kirby record 'Time of No Reply', 'Made to Love Magic', 'My Love Left With the Rain', 'The Thoughts of Mary Jane' and 'Day is Done' in the Bateman Room of Gonville and Caius College – Joe Boyd signs Nick to his Witchseason management company
July recording begins at Sound Techniques studios in Chelsea, London, on *Five Leaves Left*
October Nick moves from halls of residence at Fitzwilliam College to Handley Villa in Carlyle Road, Cambridge

1969

April Keith Morris's first photo shoot with Nick for the *Five Leaves Left* album
June Nick plays the Gonville and Caius College May Ball with Robert Kirby and orchestra – Nick plays at the Pitt Club in Cambridge
6 August Nick plays 'Time of no Reply', 'Cello Song', 'RiverMan' and 'Three Hours' for a John Peel session on BBC Radio 1
1 September release of *Five Leaves Left*

24 September Nick performs at the Royal Festival Hall in London with Fairport Convention and John and Beverley Martyn
4 October Drake performs at the Upper Room Folk Club in the Goodwill to All, in Harrow, northwest London, supported by Folkomnibus – Drake performs at The Haworth pub, Hull, East Yorkshire, supporting Michael Chapman – Drake performs at Guest, Keen and Nettlefold's Social Club, Smethwick, in the West Midlands
October Nick informs his tutor Ray Kelly that he will not be returning for his third year of study at Fitzwilliam College
15 November Nick plays at the Les Cousins club in Soho, London
December Drake plays the Coventry Apprentices Christmas Ball

1970

Nick plays a regular Saturday night spot at Les Cousins in Soho – He is known to have played at least three shows supporting the Third Ear Band, John Martyn and John James – recording begins on the *Bryter Layter* sessions
24 January Nick plays Ewell Technical College, Surrey, with Atomic Rooster and Genesis
6 February Drake performs at the Free Trade Hall in Manchester, supporting Fairport Convention
14 February Nick performs at Leicester Polytechnic supporting Genesis
21 February Performs at the Queen Elizabeth Hall, London, with John and Beverley Martyn
16 March Performs at Birmingham Town Hall supporting Fotheringay and The Humblebums
18 March Performs at De Montfort Hall in Leicester, supporting Fotheringay and The Humblebums
20 March Performs at Manchester Free Trade Hall supporting Fotheringay and The Humblebums
22 March Drake performs at Bristol Colston Hall, supporting Fotheringay and The Humblebums
30 March Drake performs at London's Royal Festival Hall, supporting Fotheringay and The Humblebums
13 April Drake's session for the BBC Radio 2 *Night Ride* programme is broadcast
8 May Performs at Bedford College, Bedford, alongside Graham Bond, Spencer Davis and John Martyn
25 June Drake plays his last live performance at Ewell Technical College, supporting Ralph McTell
Nick moves into 112 Haverstock Hill, Hampstead, London
1 November release of *Bryter Layter*

1971

March Jerry Gilbert interviews Nick Drake in *Sounds* magazine
Nick leaves London and returns to Tanworth-in-Arden
Drake stays at Chris Blackwell's villa in Algeciras in Spain
The compilation album *Nick Drake* is released in the United States, collating material from Drake's first two albums
October Two night sessions at Sound Techniques result in the *Pink Moon* album released next year
November Keith Morris conducts his last photo shoot with Nick at Hampstead Ponds
December Island Records' press officer David Sandison publishes a full-page advert in *New Musical Express* anticipating the release of *Pink Moon*
Nick contributes guitar to the recording of the *Interplay One* educational album, released the following year

1972

25 February release of *Pink Moon*
Nick suffers a breakdown and is hospitalized in Warwickshire for five weeks
Nick plays on a session for Mick Audsley at Sound Techniques

1973

John Martyn releases the album *Solid Air*, featuring the title track written about and dedicated to Nick Drake

1974

February Nick returns to Sound Techniques to record 'Black Eyed Dog', 'Hanging on a Star', 'Voice from the Mountain', 'Rider on the Wheel' and 'Tow the Line' –
Nick moves to Paris to live on a friend's houseboat for approximately six months
25 November Nick is found dead in his bedroom at Far Leys by his mother
2 December Nick's funeral service at St Mary Magdalene, Tanworth-in-Arden – his body is cremated at Solihull Crematorium
14 December Jerry Gilbert publishes 'Nick Drake – Death of a Genius' in *Sounds* magazine
18 December Dr H. Stephen Tibbits holds an inquest into Nick's death, determining suicide by self-administered Amitriptyline poisoning

1975

Nick's ashes are interred beneath an oak tree in the churchyard of St Mary Magdalene, Tanworth-in-Arden

1977

Molly and Rodney Drake give a sesquialtera stop to St Mary Magdalene's organ, dedicated to Nick and his music

1979

Drake's three albums, plus four unreleased songs from his last Sound Techniques sessions (excluding 'Tow the Line', which had yet to be discovered), are collated in a box set called *Fruit Tree*

1983

The *Fruit Tree* box set is deleted

1985

The Dream Academy has a transatlantic hit with the song 'Life in a Northern Town', dedicated to Nick Drake – release of the *Heaven in a Wild Flower* compilation album – reissue of the *Fruit Tree* box set on Joe Boyd's Hannibal imprint. The four 'final' recordings are augmented by a number of unreleased tracks and out-takes to make up a fourth disc in the box set entitled *Time of No Reply*

1986

Gorm Henrik Rasmussen publishes *Pink Moon – Sangeren og guitaristen Nick Drake* in Denmark

1987

Release of *Time Of No Reply* album as a stand-alone record

1988

Rodney Drake dies. His ashes are interred with Nick's in the churchyard of St Mary Magdalene – Molly Drake moves from Far Leys into a smaller cottage on The Green in Tanworth-in-Arden

1992

Imaginary Records release a tribute album of Nick Drake songs called *Brittle Days*, featuring artists such as Shelleyan Orphan, The Times, Loop, Scott Appel and Nikki Sudden and the French Revolution

1993

Molly Drake dies

1994

Release of *Way To Blue: An Introduction To Nick Drake* – Simon Creed publishes the first issue of the *Pynk Moon* fanzine

1997

Patrick Humphries publishes *Nick Drake: The Biography*
8 November R.E.M.'s Peter Holsapple organizes a Nick Drake tribute concert at St Ann's Church in Brooklyn, featuring Syd Straw, Peter Blegvad and Terre Roche

1998

Fruit Tree – The Nick Drake Story broadcast on BBC Radio 2

1999

1 February the documentary *A Stranger Among Us – Searching for Nick Drake*, directed by Tim Clements, is screened on the BBC
25 September Nick Drake tribute concert at The Barbican arts venue in London, featuring Robin Frederick, Beverley Martyn, Beth Orton, Bernard Butler, David Gray, Jackie Dankworth and Robyn Hitchcock
Volkswagen use 'Pink Moon' as the soundtrack for the advert for their new Cabrio car in the United States

2000

Jason Creed publishes the last issue of *Pynk Moon* after a nineteen-issue run – the documentary *A Skin Too Few: The Days of Nick Drake*, directed by Jeroen Berkvens is released

2004

Release of *Made To Love Magic* compilation album
22 May BBC Radio 2 broadcasts *Lost Boy: In Search of Nick Drake*, featuring narration by the actor Brad Pitt
May the single 'Made to love Magic' is the first Nick Drake song to reach the UK Top 40 at number 32
Release of the *Nick Drake: A Treasury* compilation album

2006

Trevor Dann publishes *Darker than the Deepest Sea: The Search for Nick Drake*

2007

Amanda Petrusich publishes *Pink Moon* for Continuum's *33⅓* series of books on classic albums
The documentary *Nick Drake: Under Review* is released by New Malden

2009

Peter Hogan publishes *Nick Drake: The Complete Guide to his Music*
16 May the tribute concert *Way to Blue: The Songs of Nick Drake* takes place at the Town Hall in Birmingham, featuring Beth Orton, Graham Coxon, Vashti Bunyan, Robyn Hitchcock and others

2010

January Joe Boyd curates four tribute concerts entitled *Way to Blue: The Songs of Nick Drake* in Manchester, Glasgow, Warwick and London, featuring Danny Thompson, Vashti Bunyan, Green Gartside, Lisa Hannigan, Scott Matthews, Teddy Thompson, Krystle Warren, Robyn Hitchcock, Kirsty Almeida and Kate St John
16 April BBC Four screens the *Way to Blue* tribute show from The Barbican in London alongside the documentary *A Skin too Few*, as part of the channel's 'Nick Drake night'

2011

Jason Creed publishes *Nick Drake: The Pink Moon Files*

2012

January Gorm Henrik Rasmussen publishes the English translation of *Pink Moon – Sangeren og guitaristen Nick Drake* in an updated edition of the 1986 original as *Pink Moon – A Story About Nick Drake*
The Idea Generation Gallery in Shoreditch, London, hosts The Strange Face Project: an exhibition of photographs taken by Michael Burdett of people listening to an unreleased version of 'Cello Song'
March Bryter Music release a CD of recordings by Molly Drake

REFERENCES

INTRODUCTION

1 *Brideshead Revisited*, dir. Charles Sturridge and Michael Lindsay-Hogg.
2 Evelyn Waugh, *Brideshead Revisited* (London, 1945).
3 Nick Drake, 'River Man', *Five Leaves Left* (London, 1969).
4 See Patrick Humphries, *Nick Drake: The Biography* (London, 1997), and Trevor Dann, *Darker than the Deepest Sea: The Search for Nick Drake* (London, 2006).
5 Born Mary Lloyd but known to her family as Molly.
6 Nick Drake, *Five Leaves Left* (London, 1969); *Bryter Layter* (London, 1970) and *Pink Moon* (London, 1972).
7 *A Stranger Among Us: In Search of Nick Drake*, dir. Tim Clements (BBC Bristol, 1999); *A Skin too Few: The Days of Nick Drake*, dir. Jeroen Berkvens, (Bonanza Films, 2000) and *Nick Drake: Under Review*, prod. Rob Johnstone (Sexy Intellectual, 2007).
8 *Lost Boy: In Search of Nick Drake*, prod. David Barber (BBC Radio 2, 2004).
9 Amanda Petrusich, *Pink Moon* (New York and London, 2007).
10 Peter Hogan, *Nick Drake: The Complete Guide to his Music* (London, 2009).
11 Jason Creed, *Nick Drake: The Pink Moon Files* (London, 2011).
12 Broadcast on 16 April 2010.
13 A post by 'Robert' on Keith James and Rick Foot's website: www. songsofnickdrake.com, accessed 11 March 2011.

1 DREAMING ENGLAND

1 London is mentioned in 'Three Hours' and 'At the Chime of a City Clock', while 'Parasite' references the Northern Line, which is a train line on the London Underground. This constitutes one specific spatial reference from each album. The most obvious reference to place again concerns London in the song 'Mayfair', not recorded for Drake's three albums but collected on the *Time of No Reply* (London, 1987) album of out-takes. The song was

subsequently recorded by the Island Records artist Millie on her *Time Will Tell* album (London, 1970).

2 Ian MacDonald, 'Nick Drake: Exiled from Heaven', *Mojo*, LXXIV (2000), p. 40.

3 Len Brown, 'Drake's Progress', *New Musical Express* (9 August 1986).

4 Mick Brown, 'The Sad Ballad of Nick Drake', *The Sunday Telegraph* (12 July 1997).

5 *English Originals*, www.algonet.se, accessed May 2011.

6 *Paul Thompson*, www.paulsongs.com, accessed 13 February 2011.

7 Mark Cooper, 'Nick Drake: Way to Blue', www.rocksbackpages.com, accessed 23 August 2010.

8 Eric Waggoner, 'The Over/Under: Nick Drake', *Magnet*, www.magnet-magazine.com, accessed 11 April 2011.

9 'Interview Joe Boyd and Vashti Bunyan', *Latest 7* (January 2010), http://thelatest.co.uk, accessed 8 May 2011.

10 John Martyn, 'Interview with Richard Skinner *Saturday Live*, Radio 1, May 25, 1986', in *Nick Drake: The Pink Moon Files*, ed. J. Creed (London, 2011), pp. 60–3.

11 Chris Jones, 'Nick Drake: *Five Leaves Left* Review', BBC Music, www.bbc.co.uk, accessed 13 February 2011.

12 Ian MacDonald, 'Nick Drake: Exiled from Heaven', *Mojo*, LXXIV (2000), p. 34.

13 Stephen Trousse, 'Goldfrapp', *Pitchfork*, http://pitchfork.com, accessed 24 October 2010.

14 Jonathan Wolff, 'Journey to Tanworth-in-Arden', in *Nick Drake: The Pink Moon Files*, ed. J. Creed (London, 2011), pp. 211–13.

15 Len Brown, 'Drake's Progress', www.rocksbackpages.com, accessed 23 August 2010, and Cooper, 'Nick Drake: Way to Blue'.

16 Nick Drake, *Family Tree* (London, 2007).

17 Barney Hoskyns, 'Nick Drake: *Family Tree* Review', www.rocksbackpages.com, accessed 23 August 2010.

18 John O'Flynn, 'National Identity and Music in Transition', in *Music, National Identity and the Politics of Location: Between the Global and the Local*, ed. I. Biddle and V. Knights (Aldershot, 2007), pp. 19–38.

19 Ernest Renan, 'What is a Nation?', in *Nation and Narration*, ed. H. K. Bhabha (London, 1990), p.11.

20 David Miller, *On Nationality* (Oxford, 1995).

21 Anthony Smith, *National Identity* (London, 1991).

22 Will Hodgkinson, *The Ballad of Britain: How Music Captured the Soul of a Nation* (London, 2009).

23 Benedict Anderson, *Imagined Communities: Reflections on the Origins and Spread of Nationalism* (London, 1991), p. 6.

24 Homi K. Bhabha, 'Introduction: Narrating the Nation', in *Nation and Narration*, ed. H. K. Bhabha (London, 1990).

25 Ian Biddle and Vanessa Knights, eds, *Music, National Identity and the Politics of Location: Between the Global and the Local* (Aldershot, 2007), see Introduction.

26 Menno Spiering, *Englishness: Foreigners and Images of National Identity in Postwar Literature* (Amsterdam, 1992), p. 8.

27 Philip V. Bohlman, 'Music and Culture: Historiographies of Disjuncture', in *The Cultural Study of Music: A Critical Introduction*, ed. M. Clayton, T. Herbert and R. Middleton (London, 2003), pp. 45–56.

28 Brian Currid 'The Acoustics of National Publicity: Music in German Mass Culture 1924–1945', PhD thesis, University of Chicago, 1998.

29 Nikolaus Pevsner, *The Englishness of English Art* (London, 1964).

30 John Barrell, 'Sir Joshua Reynolds and the Englishness of English Art', in *Nation and Narration*, ed. H. K. Bhabha (London, 1990).

31 Nathan Wiseman-Trowse, *Performing Class in British Popular Music* (Basingstoke, 2008).

32 Simon Featherstone, *Englishness: Twentieth-century Popular Culture and the Forming of English Identity* (Edinburgh, 2009).

33 Ibid., p. 10.

34 Stephen Garnett, 'The Editor's Letter', *This England*, XLIII/2 (2010), p. 33.

35 Simon Heffer, *Nor Shall my Sword: The Reinvention of England* (London, 1999), and Roger Scruton, *England: An Elegy* (London, 2000).

36 Rob Young, *Electric Eden: Unearthing Britain's Visionary Music* (London, 2010).

37 Featherstone, *Englishness*, pp. 14–15.

38 George Orwell, 'The Lion and the Unicorn', www.k-1.com, accessed August 2010, and *The English People* (London, 1947).

39 Featherstone, *Englishness*, p. 15.

40 Paul Gilroy, *'There Ain't no Black in the Union Jack': The Cultural Politics of Race and Nation* (London, 1987).

2 LISTENING TO THE LAND

1 Caitlin Moran, quoted in *Nick Drake: Under Review*, prod. Rob Johnstone, (Sexy Intellectual, 2007).

2 The lyrics do of course play a significant part in the way in which Drake's music connects to notions of Englishness. However, they will be considered in chapter Four in connection with pastoral Romantic traditions and their engagement with modernity.

3 Cally Callomon, personal email communication, 5 May 2011.

4 'Nick Drake: Five Leaves Left', in *Nick Drake: The Pink Moon Files*, ed. J. Creed (London, 2011), p. 7.
5 Jerry Gilbert, 'Nick Drake: *Bryter Layter*', in *Nick Drake: The Pink Moon Files*, p. 10.
6 Andrew Means, 'Nick Drake: *Bryter Layter*', in *Nick Drake: The Pink Moon Files*, p. 10.
7 Gilbert, 'Nick Drake: *Pink Moon*', pp. 12–13.
8 Mark Plummer, 'Nick Drake: *Pink Moon*', in *Nick Drake: The Pink Moon Files*, p. 13.
9 Joe Boyd, *White Bicycles: Making Music in the 1960s* (London, 2005), pp. 201–02.
10 An article in *Record Collector* magazine claims 'Princess of the Sand', also known as 'Strange Meeting II', as his first original composition to make it on to tape. The song was written while Drake was travelling in France and it was recorded in Aix-en-Provence in the spring of 1967. This is backed up by Robin Frederick in the liner notes to the *Family Tree* album.
11 Michael Brocken, *The British Folk Revival, 1944–2002* (Aldershot, 2003).
12 Ibid., p. 95.
13 Nick Drake shared a label with Fairport Convention and its spin-off artists Richard Thompson and Sandy Denny, as well as The Incredible String Band, Traffic and John and Beverley Martyn.
14 Brocken, *The British Folk Revival*, p. 110.
15 Ibid.
16 Nick Drake, *Family Tree* (London, 2007).
17 Dave Van Ronk, *Dave Van Ronk Sings Ballads, Blues and a Spiritual* (New York, 1959).
18 Jackson C. Frank, *Jackson C. Frank* (London, 1965).
19 Robin Frederick, 'Song of Aix', in Nick Drake, *Family Tree* (London, 2007).
20 One is tempted to make a connection between Drake's pronunciation and the land of Cockayne, a Middle Ages articulation of an English utopia present in many folk tales and songs of the period. Ray Warleigh, who plays on *Bryter Layter*, recorded an album with Soft Machine entitled *The Land of Cockayne* (London, 1981). Rob Young makes connections between Cockayne and the American folk standard 'Big Rock Candy Mountain'. See Rob Young, *Electric Eden: Unearthing Britain's Visionary Music* (London, 2010), p. 135.
21 Brian Cullman, 'Nick Drake', in *Nick Drake: The Pink Moon Files*, p. 49.
22 Kevin Ring, 'Joe Boyd and the Crazy Magic of Nick Drake', in *Nick Drake: The Pink Moon Files*, p. 84.
23 Mat Snow, 'Autumn's Child', *Mojo*, CLXXXVII (2009), p. 71.
24 Ibid., p. 70.
25 Trevor Dann, *Darker than the Deepest Sea: The Search for Nick Drake* (London,

2006), pp. 51–2.

26 Johnstone, *Nick Drake: Under Review.*

27 Dann, *Darker than the Deepest* Sea, p. 247.

28 Ian MacDonald, 'Nick Drake: Exiled from Heaven', *Mojo*, LXXIV (2000).

29 Peter Hogan, *Nick Drake: The Complete Guide to his Music* (London, 2009), p. 56.

30 A number of unofficial bootlegs exist that feature fragments of performances without vocals, both on guitar and piano. None of these have been officially released and their recording quality tends to be very poor. There are also the three instrumental tracks from *Bryter Layter* which showcase Drake's guitar playing in a relatively unadorned setting.

31 Ian MacDonald, 'Nick Drake: Exiled from Heaven', p. 40.

32 Iain Cameron, 'Minor / Major: 'River Man' and 'At the Chime of a City Clock', in *The Nick Drake Files*, www.algonet.se, accessed 30 May 2011.

33 Dann, *Darker than the Deepest Sea*, pp. 239–40.

34 Ibid., pp. 243–4.

35 'Studio Stories: Sound Techniques', in *Sound on Sound*, www.soundonsound.com, accessed 26 June 2011.

36 Ian MacDonald, 'Nick Drake: Exiled from Heaven', p. 39.

37 Simon Featherstone, *Englishness: Twentieth-century Popular Culture and the Forming of English Identity* (Edinburgh, 2009), p. 155.

38 Ibid., p. 140.

3 THE COUNTRY AND THE CITY

1 Jason Creed, 'Talking to David Sandison', in *Nick Drake: The Pink Moon Files*, ed. J. Creed (London, 2011), p. 94.

2 Trevor Dann, *Darker than the Deepest Sea: The Search for Nick Drake* (London, 2006), p. 81.

3 Gabrielle Drake quoted in Amanda Petrusich, *Pink Moon* (London, 2007), p. 27.

4 Dann, *Darker than the Deepest Sea*, p. 85.

5 Ibid., p. 103.

6 Ibid., p. 104.

7 The grounds of Marlborough College contain a prehistoric mound, locally reputed to be the grave of King Arthur's magician, Merlin. In 2011 it was carbon dated and found to be contemporary with the 5,000-year-old Silbury Hill which is 6 miles to the west. The surrounding area is one of the most archaeologically significant arrangements of stone circles, henges and long barrows in Britain. The nearby village of Avebury, situated in the heart of Europe's largest stone circle system, marks the start of the Ridgeway:

a route between the West Country and East Anglia of approximately
88 miles that is thought to be at least contemporary with Silbury and
the Marlborough mound.

8 Peter Hogan, *Nick Drake: The Complete Guide to his Music* (London, 2009), p. 32.
9 Terry Gifford, *Pastoral* (London, 1999).
10 Raymond Williams, *The Country and the City* (London, 1973), p. 1.
11 Timothy Mark Foxon, 'English Musical Pastoralism', www.musicalresources.
co.uk, accessed 8 August 2009.
12 This is with the exception of a small girl who is following her mother and
seems to be wondering what this loitering youth is up to.
13 Ian MacDonald, 'Nick Drake: Exiled from Heaven', *Mojo*, LXXIV (2000), p. 38.
14 Dann, *Darker than the Deepest Sea*, p. 65.
15 J. G. Ballard, *Concrete Island* (London, 1974).
16 Although the novel is set in 1973, it would seem to anticipate the proposed
extension of the M4 motorway into West London, which was planned but
never carried out.
17 Ballard, *Concrete Island*, p. 7.
18 Mike Bonsall, 'The Real Concrete Island', *The Ballardian*,
www.ballardian.com, accessed 24 May 2011.
19 J. G. Ballard, *The Drowned World* (New York, 1962).
20 Merlin Coverley, *Psychogeography* (Harpenden, 2006).
21 Walter Benjamin, *The Arcades Project* (Cambridge, MA, 1999).
22 *A Skin too Few: The Days of Nick Drake*, dir. Jeroen Berkvens
(Bonanza Films, 2000).
23 Chris Brazer, 'Way to Blue: A Tribute to Nick Drake', in *Nick Drake: The Pink
Moon Files*, p. 199.
24 Simon Featherstone, *Englishness: Twentieth-century Popular Culture and the
Forming of English Identity* (Edinburgh, 2009), p. 67.
25 Rob Young, *Electric Eden: Unearthing Britain's Visionary Music* (London, 2010),
p 21.
26 Lao-tzu, *Tao Te Ching*, chap. 27, http://academic. brooklyn.cuny.edu, trans.
S. Mitchell, accessed 14 June 2011.

4 MELANCHOLIA AND LOSS

1 Dr H. Stephen Tibbits quoted in Trevor Dann, *Darker than the Deepest Sea:
The Search for Nick Drake* (London, 2006), p. 190.
2 Ibid., pp. 218–19.
3 Peter Ackroyd, *Albion: The Origins of the English Imagination* (London, 2002), p. 55.

4 Ibid., p. 54.

5 Ibid., p. 57.

6 Christopher O'Riley quoted in Amanda Petrusich, *Pink Moon* (London, 2007), p. 19.

7 Robert Burton, *The Anatomy of Melancholy* (New York, 2001).

8 John Keats, 'Lamia', in *The Complete Poems of John Keats* (New York, 1994), pp. 141–56.

9 Jennifer Radden, 'Introduction: From Melancholic States to Clinical Depression', in *The Nature of Melancholy: From Aristotle to Kristeva*, ed. J. Radden (New York, 2000), p. 15.

10 John Keats, 'Ode on Melancholy', in *The Complete Poems*, pp. 194–5.

11 Ian MacDonald, 'Nick Drake: Exiled from Heaven', *Mojo*, LXXIV (2000), p. 44.

12 Petrusich, *Pink Moon*, p. 49.

13 Rodney Drake told Scott Appel that *Pink Moon* was his least favourite record of Nick's, although he and Molly loved 'From The Morning'. This was a factor that presumably led to the inscription of a line from the song on Nick's gravestone. See Patrick Humphries, *Nick Drake: The Biography* (London, 1997), p. 172.

14 Ibid., pp. 172–3.

15 Keir Keightley, 'Reconsidering Rock', in *The Cambridge Companion to Pop and Rock*, ed. S. Frith, W. Straw and J. Street (Cambridge, 2001).

16 Ibid., pp. 135–6.

17 It would be fair to point out that John Wood's production would have helped to sculpt the overall sound of the album, but given the lack of Boyd's input or that of other musicians, it is Drake's least mediated work aside from the tapes recorded at home, some of which appear on the *Family Tree* album.

18 Peter Hogan, *Nick Drake: The Complete Guide to his Music* (London, 2009), p. 55.

19 T. S. Eliot, 'The Wasteland', in *The Complete Poems and Plays of T. S. Eliot* (London, 1969), pp. 59–80.

20 Kevin Ring, 'Joe Boyd and The Crazy Magic of Nick Drake' in *Nick Drake: The Pink Moon Files*, ed. J. Creed (London, 2011), p. 84.

21 T. J. McGrath, 'Darkness Can Give You the Brightest Light', in *Nick Drake: The Pink Moon Files*, p. 210.

22 Matt Snow, 'Autumn's Child', *Mojo*, CLXXXVII (2009), p. 74.

23 Dann, *Darker than the Deepest Sea*, pp. 14–15.

24 Ibid., p. 221.

25 Ibid., p. 15.

26 Sigmund Freud, 'Mourning and Melancholia', in *Collected Papers* (London, 1967), vol. IV, pp. 152–70.

27 Jonathan Flatley, *Affective Mapping: Melancholia and the Politics of Modernism* (Cambridge, MA, 2008).

28 Julia Kristeva, *Black Sun: Depression and Melancholia*, trans. L. Roudiez (New York, 1989).

29 Flatley, *Affective Mapping*, pp. 3–4.

30 Ibid., pp. 3–4.

31 Cally Callomon quoted in Petrusich, *Pink Moon*, p. 6.

32 Ibid., p. 9.

5 DRAKE'S LEGACY

1 See Various Artists, *Interplay One* (London, 1972). Nick got the session through Robert Kirby whose girlfriend worked for Longman at the time. Drake plays guitar on three tracks: 'Full Fathom Five', 'With my Swag all on my Shoulder' (which also features Kirby singing) and 'I Wish I Was a Single Girl Again'. The album was intended to be an educational tool for secondary schools.

2 Mick Audsley, *Dark and Devil Waters* (London, 1972).

3 Millie, *Time Will Tell* (London, 1970).

4 Witchseason's publishing company.

5 John Martyn, 'Solid Air', *Solid Air* (London, 1973). The song 'He's a Poor Boy' from Witchseason labelmates Heron and its *Twice as Nice and Half the Price* album (London, 1971) also seems to suggest Nick as its subject.

6 Richard and Linda Thompson, 'Poor Boy is Taken Away', *Pour Down Like Silver* (London, 1975).

7 Nick Kent, 'Nick Drake: Requiem for a Solitary Man', *New Musical Express* (8 February 1975), pp. 14–15.

8 David Sandison, 'Nick Drake: The Final Retreat', *Zig Zag*, XLIX (1974), pp. 30–31.

9 Nick Drake, *Fruit Tree* (London, 1978).

10 The Dream Academy, 'Life In A Northern Town' (London, 1985).

11 Nick Drake, *Heaven in a Wild Flower* (London, 1985).

12 *Time of No Reply* (London, 1987).

13 *Way to Blue: An Introduction to Nick Drake* (London, 1994).

14 *Made to Love Magic* (London, 2004).

15 *A Treasury* (London, 2004).

16 *Family Tree* (London, 2007).

17 A fragment of wallpaper, attributed to Morris or one of his students, can be seen still hanging in the entrance hall to The Grove, the Regency manor house that sits within the grounds of Fitzwilliam College, Cambridge. The Grove is now home to the Senior Common Room and houses some of the

College's fellows, but was owned by Emma Darwin, wife of the naturalist Charles Darwin, between 1883 and 1896. Emma Darwin had the house decorated in the Arts and Crafts style.

18 On the original image the billboard says: 'BUDGET SPEECH', echoing the imminent budget to be announced by Roy Jenkins on the day of the photo shoot, 29 April 1969.

19 Trevor Dann, *Darker than the Deepest Sea: The Search for Nick Drake* (London, 2006), p. 209.

20 The advertisement shares a striking similarity to the work of Christo and Jeanne-Claude, who have created site-specific artworks involving the wrapping or draping of cloth over landscapes and landmarks. AT&T were forced to put a disclaimer at the end of the advert assuring that there was no connection between them and the artists.

21 Dann, *Darker than the Deepest Sea*, p. 210.

22 Although it has not been officially released, the song is available to download at www.spin.com.

23 Danny Cavanagh, *A Place To Be: A Tribute To Nick Drake* (London, 2004).

24 Available as an extra track on the Japanese pressing of The Mars Volta's fourth album *The Bedlam in Goliath* (Los Angeles, 2008).

25 Drive, 'Road' on *Out Freakage* (Wigan, 1992), and Sebadoh, 'Pink Moon', on *Smash Your Head on the Punk Rock* (Seattle, 1992).

26 These tracks were streamed on Beck's website in 2006 but were not officially released.

27 Lucinda Williams, 'Which Will', on *Sweet Old World* (New York, 1992).

28 Recorded with The Charlie Hunter Band and released as the B-side of the single release of Nick Drake's 'River Man' (London, 2004), released to coincide with the BBC Radio 2 documentary *Lost Boy: In Search of Nick Drake*.

29 Brad Meldhau, 'River Man' *The Art of the Trio*, vol. III (Burbank, CA, 1998), and Christopher O'Riley, *Second Grace: The Music of Nick Drake* (Burbank, 2007).

30 Norma Waterson, on 'River Man' *The Very Thought of You* (New York, 2002).

31 Rachel Unthank and the Winterset, 'River Man', *Cruel Sister* (London, 2005).

32 Recorded for the Island Records compilation *Island Life: 50 Years of Island Records* (London, 2009) and subsequently released as the B-side to his single 'No Tears to Cry' (London, 2010).

33 Natacha Atlas, 'River Man' on *Mounqaliba* (Burbank, 2010).

34 Gorm Henrik Rasmussen, *Pink Moon: A Story about Nick Drake* (London, 2012).

35 George Orwell, 'The Lion and the Unicorn', www.k-1.com, accessed 23 August 2010.

SELECT BIBLIOGRAPHY

Ackroyd, Peter, Albion: *The Origins of the English Imagination* (London, 2002)

Adams, Richard, *Watership Down* (London, 1972)

Anderson, Benedict, *Imagined Communities: Reflections on the Origins and Spread of Nationalism* (London, 1991)

Ballard, J. G., *The Drowned World* (New York, 1962)

——, *Concrete Island* (London, 1974)

Baucom, Ian, *Out of Place: Englishness, Empire, and the Locations of Identity*, (Princeton, NJ, 1999)

Benjamin, Walter, *The Arcades Project* (Cambridge, MA, 1999)

Bhabha, Homi K, ed., *Nation and Narration* (London, 1990)

Biddle, Ian, and Vanessa Knights, eds, *Music, National Identity and the Politics of Location: Between the Global and the Local* (Aldershot, 2007)

Boyd, Joe, *White Bicycles: Making Music in the 1960s* (London, 2005)

Brocken, Michael, *The British Folk Revival, 1944–2002* (Aldershot, 2003)

Burke, Kathleen, ed., *The British Isles Since 1945* (Oxford, 2003)

Burton, Robert, *The Anatomy of Melancholy* (New York, 2001)

Camus, Albert, *The Myth of Sisyphus* (London, 2005)

Clayton, Martin, Trevor Herbert and Richard Middleton, eds, *The Cultural Study of Music: A Critical Introduction* (London, 2003)

Colls, Robert, *Identity of England* (Oxford, 2002)

Coverley, Merlin, *Psychogeography* (Harpenden, 2006)

Creed, Jason, *Nick Drake: The Pink Moon Files* (London, 2011)

Currid, Brian, 'The Acoustics of National Publicity: Music in German Mass Culture 1924–1945', PhD thesis. University of Chicago, 1998

Dann, Trevor, *Darker than the Deepest Sea: The Search for Nick Drake* (London, 2006)

Defoe, Daniel, *Robinson Crusoe* (London, 1966)

——, *A Journal of the Plague Year* (London, 2003)

Donnelly, Mark, *Sixties Britain* (Harlow, 2005)

Du Noyer, Paul, *In the City: A Celebration of London Music* (London, 2009)

Eliot, T. S., *The Complete Poems and Plays of T. S. Eliot* (London, 1969)

Enterline, Lynn, *The Tears of Narcissus: Melancholia and Masculinity in Early Modern Writing* (Stanford, CA, 1995)

Faulk, Barry J., *British Rock Modernism, 1967–1977* (Farnham, 2010)

Featherstone, Simon, *Englishness: Twentieth-Century Popular Culture and the Forming of English Identity* (Edinburgh, 2009)

Flatley, Jonathan, *Affective Mapping: Melancholia and the Politics of Modernism* (Cambridge, MA, 2008)

Foxon, Timothy Mark, 'English Musical Pastoralism', www.musicalresources.co.uk, accessed 8 August 2009.

Freud, Sigmund, *Collected Papers*, vol. IV (London, 1967)

Frith, Simon, Will Straw and John Street, eds, *The Cambridge Companion to Pop and Rock* (Cambridge, 2001)

Gifford, Terry, *Pastoral* (London, 1999)

Gilroy, Paul, 'There Ain't no Black in the Union Jack': The Cultural Politics of Race and Nation* (London, 1987)

Green, Jonathon, *All Dressed Up: The Sixties and the Counterculture* (London, 1999)

Heffer, Simon, *Nor Shall my Sword: The Reinvention of England* (London, 1999)

Hodgkinson, Will, *The Ballad of Britain: How Music Captured the Soul of a Nation* (London, 2009)

Hogan, Peter, *Nick Drake: The Complete Guide to his Music* (London, 2009)

Humphries, Patrick, *Nick Drake: The Biography* (London, 1997)

Keats, John, *The Complete Poems of John Keats* (New York, 2000)

Kristeva, Julia, *Black Sun: Depression and Melancholia*, trans. L. Roudiez (New York, 1989)

Lawrence, D. H., *Lady Chatterley's Lover* (London, 2010)

Leoussi, Athena S., and Steven Grosby, *Nationalism and Ethnosymbolism: History, Culture and Ethnicity in the Formation of Nations* (Edinburgh, 2007)

Matless, David, *Landscape and Englishness* (London, 1998)

Mellers, Wilfrid, *Vaughan Williams and the Vision of Albion* (London, 1989)

Miller, David, *On Nationality* (Oxford, 1995)

Morton, H. V., *In Search of England*, (London, 1927)

Munro, John Neil, *Some People are Crazy: The John Martyn Story* (Edinburgh, 2007)

Nairn, Tom, *After Britain: New Labour and the Return of Scotland* (Cambridge, 2000)

Orwell, George, *The English People* (London, 1947)

——, 'The Lion and the Unicorn', www.k-1.com, accessed 23 August 2010.

Petrusich, Amanda, *Pink Moon* (New York and London, 2007)

Pevsner, Nikolaus, *The Englishness of English Art* (London, 1964)
Poe, Edgar Allan, *The Penguin Edgar Allan Poe* (London, 1995)
Radden, Jennifer, ed., *The Nature of Melancholy: From Aristotle to Kristeva*
    (New York, 2000)
Rasmussen, Gorm Henrik, *Pink Moon: A Story About Nick Drake* (London, 2012)
Scruton, Roger, *England: An Elegy* (London, 2000)
Smith, Anthony, *National Identity* (London, 1991)
Spiering, Menno, *Englishness: Foreigners and Images of National Identity in Postwar
    Literature* (Amsterdam, 1992)
Waugh, Evelyn, *Brideshead Revisited* (London, 1945)
White, Jerry, *London in the Twentieth Century* (London, 2002)
Williams, Raymond, *The Country and the City* (London, 1973)
Wiseman-Trowse, Nathan, *Performing Class in British Popular Music*
    (Basingstoke, 2008)
Young, Rob, *Electric Eden: Unearthing Britain's Visionary Music* (London, 2010)

DISCOGRAPHY

Below are the official studio albums and compilations released in Nick Drake's name. Bootleg recordings exist that feature other pieces or unreleased versions of his songs, but at the time of writing they have yet to be made public in any official capacity.

Five Leaves Left
1969, ILPS9105
'Time Has Told Me', 'River Man', 'Three Hours', 'Way to Blue', 'Day is Done', 'Cello Song', 'The Thoughts of Mary Jane', 'Man in a Shed', 'Fruit Tree', 'Saturday Sun'.

Bryter Layter
1970, ILPS9134
'Introduction', 'Hazey Jane II', 'At the Chime of a City Clock', 'One of these Things First', 'Hazey Jane I', 'Bryter Layter', 'Fly', 'Poor Boy', 'Northern Sky', 'Sunday'.

Pink Moon
1972, ILPS9184
'Pink Moon', 'Place to Be', 'Road', 'Which Will', 'Horn', 'Things Behind the Sun', 'Know', 'Parasite', 'Free Ride', 'Harvest Breed', 'From the Morning'

Fruit Tree
1979, NDSP100
Island Records' retrospective box set includes the three studio albums, with the songs 'Rider on the Wheel', 'Black Eyed Dog', 'Hanging on a Star' and 'Voice from the Mountain' added at the end of the *Pink Moon* disc.

Heaven in a Wild Flower
1985, ILPS9826
Compiled by Trevor Dann and Nick Stewart
'Fruit Tree', 'Cello Song', 'Thoughts of Mary Jane', 'Northern Sky', 'River Man',
'At the Chime of a City Clock', 'Introduction', 'Hazey Jane I', 'Hazey Jane II',
'Pink Moon', 'Road', 'Which Will', 'Things Behind the Sun', 'Time Has Told Me'

Fruit Tree
1986, HNBX5302
The Hannibal version of the *Fruit Tree* set returns *Pink Moon* to its original track
list and includes a fourth disc, titled *Time of no Reply*, including the four 'last'
tracks, plus unreleased songs and alternative takes (see below).

Time of no Reply
1987, HNBL1318
The fourth disc from the Hannibal *Fruit Tree* box set is given a stand-alone
release.
'Time of No Reply', 'I Was Made to Love Magic', 'Joey', 'Clothes of Sand', 'Man
in a Shed', 'Mayfair', 'Fly', 'The Thoughts of Mary Jane', 'Been Smoking Too
Long', 'Strange Meeting II', 'Rider on the Wheel', 'Black Eyed Dog', 'Hanging on
a Star', 'Voice From the Mountain'

Way to Blue: An Introduction to Nick Drake
1994, IMCD196
Compiled by Joe Boyd.
'Cello Song', 'Hazey Jane I', 'Way to Blue', 'Things Behind the Sun', 'River Man',
'Poor Boy', 'Time of No Reply', 'From the Morning', 'One of These Things
First', 'Northern Sky', 'Which Will', 'Hazey Jane II', 'Time Has Told Me', 'Pink
Moon', 'Black Eyed Dog', 'Fruit Tree'.

Made to Love Magic
2004, CID8141
Comprising unreleased versions of several staples of Nick's catalogue including
Robert Kirby's original orchestrations of 'Magic' and 'Time of No Reply'
recorded in 2003 and mixed with original music and vocals. The album also
includes the lost track 'Tow the Line' from Nick's final recording session. 'Rider
on the Wheel', 'Magic', 'River Man', 'Joey', 'The Thoughts of Mary Jane',
'Mayfair', 'Hanging on a Star', 'Three Hours', 'Clothes of Sand', 'Voices' ('Voice
From The Mountain'), 'Time of No Reply', 'Black Eyed Dog', 'Tow the Line'.

A Treasury

2004, CID8149

This compilation features a brief extract of Nick playing 'Plaisir d'Amour'. Otherwise, it closely duplicates *Way To Blue*.

'Introduction', 'Hazey Jane II', 'River Man', 'Cello Song', 'Hazey Jane I', 'Pink Moon', 'Poor Boy', 'Magic', 'Place to Be', 'Northern Sky', 'Road', 'Fruit Tree', 'Black Eyed Dog', 'Way to Blue', 'From the Morning', 'Plaisir d'Amour'.

Family Tree

2007, 1734041

A compilation of material recorded at Far Leys, Cambridge and Aix-en-Provence, some of which had been available as sonically inferior bootlegs. The album was compiled and produced by Cally Callomon and remastered by John Wood.

'Come into the Garden', They're Leaving Me Behind', 'Time Piece', 'Poor Mum' (performed by Molly Drake), 'Winter is Gone', 'All My Trials' (performed by Nick and Gabrielle Drake), 'Mozart's Kegelstatt Trio' (performed by Nick on clarinet and his aunt and uncle Nancy and Chris McDowall on viola and piano), 'Strolling Down the Highway', 'Paddling in Rushmere', 'Cocaine Blues', 'Blossom', 'Been Smoking too Long', 'Black Mountain Blues', 'Tomorrow is a Long Time', If You Leave Me', 'Here Comes the Blues', 'Sketch I', 'Blues Run the Game', 'My Baby so Sweet', 'Milk and Honey', 'Kimbie', 'Bird Flew By', 'Rain', 'Strange Meeting II', 'Day is Done', 'Come into the Garden', 'Way to Blue', 'Do You Ever Remember?' (performed by Molly Drake).

ACKNOWLEDGEMENTS

Many people have assisted me in the planning and writing of this book. To begin with, I would like to thank John Scanlan and Lee Marshall for giving me the chance to write it. I would also like to thank Michael and Harry at Reaktion for their invaluable help and guidance in putting the finished work together. I am extremely grateful to Cally Callomon at Bryter Music and Dr Terry Rogers at Marlborough College for their time and the insights that they gave me into Nick's life and music. They have both been of repeated assistance throughout the research and writing process and it has been a pleasure to meet two real English gentlemen. I would also like to thank Dr Paul Chirico, Professor David Thompson and Alison Carter, who kindly showed me around Fitzwilliam College, as well as Dave Barber and Anne Joynt for their invaluable contributions and details. My colleagues at The University of Northampton have been a constant source of support and help and I would particularly like to thank Richard Hollingum, Dr Lawrence Phillips, Ted Sullivan, Dr Lorna Jowett, Dr Stephen Keane, Professor Jeff Ollerton, Dr Phillippa Bennett, Dr Sonya Andermahr and Dr Jennifer Skellington for their thoughts, contributions and support, as well as Paul Middleton and Professor Janet Wilson for arranging some much-needed research leave. I would also like to thank my Music and Identity students (2010/2011) who helped me thrash out the ideas that shaped this book. Particular thanks should go to Dr Mike Starr and Dr Carlo Nardi, who listened to me rant about Drake for almost two years and provided a vital sounding-board. Thanks go to the members of IASPM who helped me out on the accent, Professor Sheila Whiteley for assuring me I was on the right track. Particular thanks go to John Williamson and Dr Christophe Pirenne for helping me out in a tight spot. Much gratitude goes to Paul Drummond, Libby Chisman, Mark Jones, Lisa Richards and Clare Morris for helping me out with the images. I am of course eternally grateful to Paul Hillery for his beautiful photographs and his help and contributions throughout the process. Finally, I would also like to thank Mark Thorneycroft, Nic Blanch, Bob Fletcher, Andres Romero Jodar, John Sinclair of Aylesbury, Buckinghamshire, the Trowses and the Wisemans.

But above all, thank you, Kelly, for keeping me going, listening to my nonsense and looking after the bairn when I was camped out in the shed. I could not have done it without you.

Oh, and Nick, thanks for the songs, I am still not sick of them.

PHOTO ACKNOWLEDGEMENTS

The author and the publishers wish to express their thanks to the below sources of illustrative material and / or permission to reproduce it:

Courtesy of Getty Images: pp. 6, 18, 95 (photos Keith Morris 1970); photos © Paul Hillery 2011: pp. 11, 25, 35, 41, 61, 69, 81, 82; Courtesy Island Records: pp. 55, 87; Courtesy Marlborough College Archives: pp. 73, 75, 77; Photo Hege Saebjornsen: p. 131.

INDEX